Keep Your Bonsai Alive & Well

Herb L. Gustafson

Sterling Publishing Co., Inc. New York

Library of Congress Cataloging-in-Publication Data

Gustafson, Herb L.
    Keep your bonsai alive & well / by Herb L. Gustafson.
        p.   cm.
    Includes index.
    ISBN 0-8069-1310-X
    1. Bonsai.   I. Title.   II. Title: Keep your bonsai alive and
well.
  SB433.5.G873   1995
  635.9'772—dc20   94-42923
                                                              CIP

10   9   8   7   6   5   4   3   2   1

Published by Sterling Publishing Company, Inc.
387 Park Avenue South, New York, N.Y. 10016
© 1995 by Herb L. Gustafson
Distributed in Canada by Sterling Publishing
% Canadian Manda Group, One Atlantic Avenue, Suite 105
Toronto, Ontario, Canada M6K 3E7
Distributed in Great Britain and Europe by Cassell PLC
Wellington House, 125 Strand, London WC2R 0BB, England
Distributed in Australia by Capricorn Link (Australia) Pty Ltd.
P.O. Box 6651, Baulkham Hills, Business Centre,
NSW 2153, Australia
Printed in Hong Kong
All rights reserved

Sterling ISBN 0-8069-1310-X

ACKNOWLEDGMENTS

I'd like to thank my wife, Susan Y. Gustafson, for her countless hours of compiling, editing, alphabetizing, and word processing. Thanks to Randall M. MacLean-Kennedy for the discussion, philosophy and distracting pleasantries necessary for me to complete any task. To Dick McRill, photographer, for his patience with me. Thanks to Greg and Sue Wilson at *The Indoor Garden* for the signings and the use of their wonderful facilities and plant material. To Aleta, for her constant accommodation, and to J.R. for teaching me how to work.

Special thanks to Charles G. Nurnberg for the idea for this work. I hope this book fills a critical gap in bonsai literature.

CONTENTS

PREFACE... 4

1. OUTDOORS OR INDOORS?.................. 5

2. WATERING... 11

3. WEEDING.. 17

4. SUMMER CARE 20

5. WINTER CARE 27

6. REPOTTING 31

7. INSECTS 39

8. DISEASES 47

9. SOILS & FERTILIZERS.......................... 52

10. EMERGENCY TREATMENT...................... 57

11. SEASONAL CHECKLIST 63

12. APPENDIX.. 85

INDEX.. 96

PREFACE

For almost forty years I've answered questions about bonsai. It seems remarkable that out of all the possible problems one might encounter in this fascinating hobby, most inquiries deal with the basic survival of the plant! It seems the more esoteric the problem, the less likely it is to present itself. Perhaps there are thousands of potential questions I might be asked, yet I seem to be asked the same thirty questions.

This book attempts to answer those thirty questions, and more. In any educational endeavor, we're all aware of the increased curiosity that comes as the result of knowledge. I will attempt to anticipate future questions, as well. Above all, survival of the bonsai comes before design implications.

The bonsai grower takes on an obligation to fulfill the biological needs of the plant. I hope this book will be a cornerstone in building your confidence and your bonsai collection.

Chapter 1

OUTDOORS OR INDOORS?

Well-meaning individuals try to grow a juniper bonsai on their coffee table. A pine tree slowly withers on top of the television set. A florist azalea turns black on the picnic table outside.

These sad occurrences don't have to happen. If you buy a bonsai, pay careful attention to the location in which it was growing. These bonsai are growing inside the store. Beautiful windows and skylights allow ample light to stream in and provide energy for the growth of these bonsai. **Fig. 1-1.** Most florist shops sell indoor bonsai. Most garden nurseries sell outdoor bonsai. Lattice-work and the metal screening provide both shade and security for these outdoor bonsai. **Fig. 1-2.** If there is any question at all, feel free to ask the shopkeeper. Additional growing information is usually provided as a hand-out, brochure or instruction label. Read these materials carefully. If there

are still any questions in your mind, contact one of the members of a local bonsai society or garden club.

With the recent burgeoning interest in bonsai comes a variety of bonsai available—not all of them real. Bonsai can now be found that are made of silk, paper, silver wire, plastic and other sturdy materials. A new product, quite convincing in appearance, is a pre-served plant. Typically a juniper, it's quite green and flexible and planted in a plastic bonsai container. A naive cus-tomer or gift recipient might actually believe that this plant will thrive and grow.

With a variety of stores supplying bonsai and bonsai material, it becomes imperative that the purchaser get a positive identification of the plant. If the identity isn't known, it will also be difficult to know how to care for the plant. I've seen bonsai for sale at out-

Fig. 1-1

Fig. 1-2

door markets, grocery stores, department stores and variety shops. In these establishments, the bonsai might have been placed on a shelf only temporarily; the plant's surroundings might not indicate the best environment for successful growing.

Avoid using common names. A Norfolk Island pine isn't a pine; a Hinoki cypress isn't a cypress; a Chinese Snow Rose isn't a rose. The common name for a plant is sometimes misleading. Most serious gardeners use the plant's Latin name. To ensure accurate information for the reader, this book refers to the Latin name wherever practical.

What follows is a partial plant list by common name that includes most of the larger groups of plants suitable for bonsai; it is by no means a complete list. For a complete list, see chapter 12. Most bonsai plants can be grouped into one of three environmental classifications: outdoor bonsai, partially outdoor bonsai and indoor bonsai.

OUTDOOR BONSAI

Outdoor bonsai are typically conifers, **Fig. 1-3,** broadleaf evergreens, **Fig. 1-4,** and deciduous trees, **Fig. 1-5,** native to colder climates. These hardy trees and shrubs are subject to freezing temperatures every winter in their natural habitats. As bonsai, they'll tolerate some freezing temperatures overnight. The variety of plants in this classification is large, accounting for most bonsai species. **Fig. 1-6.** Included in this group are: pine, **Fig. 1-7,** juniper, **Fig. 1-8,** hemlock, spruce, fir, **Fig. 1-9,** cedar, rhododendron, azalea, alder, hornbeam, birch, beech, camel-

Fig. 1-3

Fig. 1-6

Fig. 1-4

Fig. 1-7

Fig. 1-5

Fig. 1-8

Fig. 1-10

lia, quince, dogwood, redbud, cypress, hawthorn, larch, **Fig. 1-10,** filbert, cherry, pear, oak, willow, arborvitae.

PARTIALLY OUTDOOR BONSAI

Partially outdoor bonsai are native to temperate climates. While it may sometimes freeze in their local environment, it isn't necessary that the potted tree be subject to these cold temperatures. Typically a bonsai grower will move the plant about as climatic changes dictate. The bonsai is placed in the shade outdoors in April. **Fig. 1-11.** The plant spends the summer cooling in the breezes under the canopy of a large tree. When the first frosts arrive, the tree becomes an indoor bonsai, in a sunny location in the home. Some good examples of these plants are: evergreen oaks, evergreen maples, Chinese elm, **Fig. 1-12,** Japanese green-mound juniper, **Fig. 1-13,** Kingsbury boxwood, Chinese tea, pomegranate, bamboo, Montezuma cypress, bald cypress, buttonwood, peach, citrus, jade, succulent pine, fuchsia, magnolia, olive, palm, Seiju elm, **Fig. 1-14,** Hokkaido elm, Chinese Snow Rose, **Fig. 1-15,** Chinese date tree.

Fig. 1-11

Fig. 1-12

Fig. 1-13

Fig. 1-14

Fig. 1-15

INDOOR BONSAI

Indoor bonsai are made from tropical plants. Florist shops sell these indoor plants that are native to the tropical regions of Africa, Asia, and South America. Small-leaved varieties are most often utilized due to the usually enormous sizes of leaves found in these lush regions. The bonsai is usually placed in a well lit location that has adequate ventilation. **Fig. 1-16.** In warmer climates, these bonsai may be brought outside for a limited time in

Fig. 1-16

Fig. 1-17

full shade. Some plants that are often utilized are: figs, **Fig. 1-17,** schefflera, aralia, **Fig. 1-18,** cycas, kalanchoe, pelargonium, succulents, cacti, portulacaria, hibiscus, fatshedera, crassula, hedera, nerium, pilea, poinsettia, bougainvillea.

I hope this brief overview will correct a common misconception. Most bonsai exhibits are found indoors, in convention centers, malls and art galleries. Unfortunately, beginners to the horticulture of bonsai start off thinking that all bonsai are indoor plants. Indeed, this is where they look fabulous. Most bonsai are outdoor plants. If you must have an indoor bonsai, simply pot and train an indoor plant. If you purchase a finished bonsai, be aware of its needs. A tropical plant doesn't have to feel the seasons, for there are none in its native habitat. Such a plant only needs lots of indirect light, consistent moisture, and moderate heat. Outdoor plants, by contrast, need to feel the passage of the seasons in order to set their internal biological clocks. Such plants depend heavily on the height, location and duration of the sun to create winter, spring, summer, and fall, just as all plants do that are native to colder climates. Satisfy the needs of the plant and the bonsai will satisfy you in return.

Fig. 1-18

Chapter 2

WATERING

Fig. 2-1. When my bonsai teacher finally handed me his watering can after months of training, I knew I'd graduated. With that simple gesture, he was trusting me with the lives of his masterpieces, his grandfather's bonsai as well as his future grandchildren's bonsai. Watering isn't a small task, to be taken lightly. With a careful eye to the moisture content in the container, you can control growth, inhibit insects, prevent disease and monitor the general development of your tree. Water isn't just wetness in the pot, it's the lifeblood of the plant. Water carries nutrients, helps the plant breathe in summer, and transports growth hormones. Water provides the turgor pressure necessary to keep new growth upright. Water keeps the plant flexible so it can turn towards the sun and align itself with the seasons. The horticulture of bonsai, as with any plant, is complex and intertwined. Water provides the means of transport for biochemical processes, without which all systems fail. Osmotic communications between living cells cease to function without water. **Fig. 2-2.**

Plants growing in the ground have a large volume of earth from which to draw their necessary moisture; the potted plant has no such "reserve." **Fig. 2-3.** Once the bonsai is dry, it's desperately dry. The plant in the ground can rely on deeper roots for sustenance in warmer weather. The volume of a bonsai pot just doesn't allow for a so-called "tap root," so careful attention to watering bonsai is critical. By confining the roots in an enclosed container, you've committed yourself to providing the plant with all its needs. If that obligation is too demanding of your time and attention, simply plant the bonsai back in the ground for a few days, or a few years. The bonsai can always be repotted later. Better a live potential bonsai growing in the ground than a dead bonsai in a beautiful pot! **Fig. 2-4.**

Fig. 2-5 shows a moisture-content

Fig. 2-1

Fig. 2-3

Fig. 2-2

Fig. 2-4

graph. This graph will help you understand the concepts discussed in this chapter. The bottom horizontal line represents the passing of time from point zero to some point in the future. The actual time varies with the size of the pot, vigor of the plant, the temperature of the surroundings and other

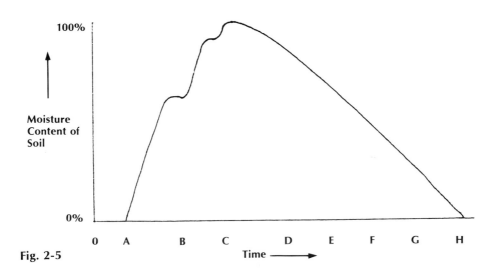

Moisture
Content of
Soil

100%

0%

0   A   B   C   D   E   F   G   H

Time ⟶

Fig. 2-5

factors, such as wind velocity, humidity and the like. Thus, the time from A to H could be as little as three hours, or as much as a week. The vertical line on the left represents the percentage of moisture in the bonsai soil that's in your container.

At Time A, the soil is lightly watered with a fine mist. This watering takes just a few seconds. Notice the immediate rise in moisture content. Water trickles along the surface of the soil, along the edges of the pot and out through the drain holes in the bottom of the pot. Some water has penetrated between the soil particles and has made its way to the bottom of the container as well, but the particles remain partially dry.

Leave the bonsai alone for ten or fifteen minutes. Continuous watering at this point would be futile. The dryness of the soil particles creates a repulsion to water due to the surface tension of the water itself. The soil particles, as well as the container, are able to make the water microscopically "bead up" and be temporarily rejected. After a few minutes this surface tension relaxes as the soil particles become wet.

At Time B, a few minutes after Time A, the soil is ready to receive additional moisture. A good thorough sprinkling or soaking at this time drenches the soil particles, and the moisture content in the soil reaches almost 100%. All soil particles are wet. The inside as well as the outside of the container is wet. The excess water flows freely through the pot's drain holes, and air is sucked down from above by the action of the retreating water as it channels through the soil. Well-draining bonsai soil will

actually make a soft sound like a slide whistle, with its slide being pulled down at a moderate speed. As water is pulled down by gravity, air is pulled behind it into the small channels between soil particles. The resulting subtle descending glissando is a sure sign of perfectly made bonsai soil. Listen for it.

Between Time B and Time C, an important process occurs that takes about ten minutes. The flood of water in the soil dislodges dust, fills minor crevices and dissolves minerals and salts in the soil. During this period, an equilibrium is reached. The osmotic pressure around the soil particles begins to equal the osmotic pressure inside the root hairs of the plant. Ion exchange begins, and the waste products are disposed of, nutrient stores are inventoried and adjusted. Storage organs are cleaned and purged of unnecessary or redundant supplies.

An additional watering at Time C is a bonus to the plant. Excess mineral byproducts and harmful salts are disposed of rapidly in the presence of water-saturated soil. Dry soil will force the plant to retain these harmful wastes. By watering again at Time C, you don't increase the moisture content in the soil significantly. You accomplish something more important: You take out the garbage. Miss this third watering and your plant won't perform well.

You'll notice by looking at the graph that the water content of the soil gradually decreases towards zero at Time H. This decrease is due to evaporation, transpiration within the plant itself and, of course, the growth of the root tips. At some point (Time G), there's insufficient water in the pot available to the plant. At Time G, there's still some residual moisture left in the pot, but it's of no use to the plant.

We often hear the expressions, "Keep this plant a little on the dry side," or "Keep moist at all times." The time designations D, E, F, G, and H are designed to clarify just what those instructions mean.

At Time D, the surface of the soil is wet. There's no dryness seen. The total moisture content has dropped considerably from Time C, but there are no visible or tactile signs that the soil surface has dried out in any way. For some plants native to the world's darkest, steamiest rain forests, this is the time to begin the watering cycle all over again. For this select group of plants, begin at Time A again and don't forget Times B and C. One watering cycle is defined by three individual waterings, at times A, B and C, in that order. Depending upon the individual species, proceed to D, E, F, G or perhaps (in the case of cactus) even H. Correct watering always begins with the three initial waterings, then proceeds to locate the proper time to begin the sequence again. This might be at D, or at some other point in time.

Plants that need to be watered at Time E differ from the plants that need to be watered at Time D. These plants at E are usually found growing in deep topsoil formed by decomposing leaves or needles from larger trees above them. Some common examples are the African violet, azalea, fern and deepwoods wildflower. Wait to see surface drying in the bonsai container before watering. The surface-soil particles not only display a lightened color, but they're dry to the touch.

Those plants that prefer to be watered at Time F are "average" plants. This group contains most bonsai plants, such as conifers, deciduous trees, broadleaf evergreens, and the like. The soil surface is allowed to dry and then a little more time is added. At Time F, the pot is a bit lighter in the hands, yet still cool to the touch. A probing finger still finds moisture below the surface. There's no visible wilt to the foliage. For most pots, if Time D is reached in, say, two days, Time F will be reached in about four days. This actual time is quite relative and very variable, depending upon other conditions.

Plants that like to be watered at Time G are a hardy group of alpine, subalpine, arctic and semiarid plants. Some plants in this group are the high-desert junipers, subalpine fir, piñon pine, palm and arctic birch. Before beginning again with the watering sequence A, B and C, look for the following signs: No noticeable moisture in the container when poked with the finger; the container is light in weight and warm from the sun; surface dryness has disappeared for some time. The plant's bark is dry, brittle and grey, as naturally bleached by the sun; there are no drops of moisture near the drain holes of the container; the soil in the container has contracted slightly so that a small gap is visible between the root ball and the container.

Some plants like to be watered even less frequently than does the previous group. Such plants have their own internal water-storage containers. These plants like to be watered at Time H. They include the typical cactus, the succulent family of related plants; the Travelers palm, the baobab tree of East Africa, the saltwater-tolerant portulacas and the amazing array of alpine and low-desert plants that seem to thrive on neglect! Time H is characterized by the complete absence of moisture. The pot is hot to the touch; it's dry and lightweight. A probing fingertip uncovers no dark soil particles, nor feels cool soil. The plant may have dropped some or all of its leaves as a moisture conservation effort. This leaf loss is normal for this group of plants.

One aspect of watering that's often ignored is attention to the quality of water. If after several months of A, B, C type watering, you still see white mineral deposits accumulated on the inside rim of the pot, you may have a highly mineral water supply and you'll have to store your water in a container before using it. A large water vessel of some kind can be used to settle out minerals and evaporate high amounts of chlorine and related elements. Standing water is always safer for bonsai than water directly from the tap or well. In Japanese nurseries, the traditional copper watering can is dipped into a large ceramic or oak vessel and the water is carried to each individual plant. **Fig. 2-6.** If your water seems to

be having an adverse effect on your trees, various governmental agencies near you can test your water, usually for a modest fee.

For most purposes, using tap water from a hose seems to be the watering method of choice. **Fig. 2-7.** There are watering nozzles (available from nurseries) that spread the water out into fine droplets that neither harm the plant nor wash away the soil. The rose

Fig. 2-7

at the end of the Japanese bonsai watering can has been modified for hose-end use. This rose is what I prefer. There are also countless watering devices with built-in shut-off valves and pressure regulators. Try to select a device that best suits your individual needs and applications.

There are also numerous automated systems available, intended to simplify your bonsai-watering schedule. These systems have several things in common. They're a bit more expensive than simple nozzles, watering cans or sprinklers; they require a bit of planning and setup, and they'll all fail at some time or another. Nurseries with elaborate watering systems costing tens of thousands of dollars still have to call the plumber once in a while. An automatic watering system can be a useful

Fig. 2-6

tool if purchased and used with a healthy dose of mechanical knowledge, constant observation and humor. If a squirrel decides that your miniature water emitter is in its way, it will simply move it. If your bonsai dies subsequently, it wasn't the squirrel's fault, it was because you didn't get out and closely observe your system.

Pipes freeze, water lines burst, fittings leak, solenoids fail, electricity will be interrupted. Ultimately, the responsibility and the success of your watering schedule still depends upon you. I find that the quiet time with my trees is something I look forward to; I don't consider watering to be an inconvenience.

Chapter 3

WEEDING

One wouldn't think that weeding, or more specifically, lack of weeding, could seriously affect the life of a bonsai. Weeds are just plants that we wish would grow somewhere else. Unfortunately, the most prolific and well-known weeds are those plants that compete successfully with what we're trying to grow. If we nurture our bonsai properly, we'll eventually find a weed in the pot that grows just fine under those conditions. **Fig. 3-1.** Remove these pests as soon as possible, while their root systems are still small. Once a major weed, such as a thistle, gets its roots tangled up with your favorite pine-bonsai roots, you'll have to repot the whole tree; otherwise the thistle will regrow in just a few days.

Weeds compete favorably with bonsai. They rob nutrition from the soil that's intended for the tree. Weeds shade the roots of the bonsai, causing the bonsai to sulk. Weeds detract from the appearance of the plant; they harbor insects and disease. They even at-tract them!

Some weeds indicate poor soil conditions. The common liverwort, **Fig. 3-2,** appears only when certain environmental circumstances are present. When you see this weed, look for poor-draining soil. Check to see that there's no rotting humus in your soil to interfere with its breathing pores. This weed is often seen when high-nitrogen fertilizers or time-release capsules have been applied to the soil surface. A word of caution: Time-release fertilizers are dependent on higher temperatures as well as on time. Heavy application of these fertilizers to the soil without adequate water flushing will encourage the formation of green slime. Liverwort thrives in such an environment. See chapter 9.

Irish moss, and its close companion, Scotch moss, make nice ground covers in the garden. **Fig. 3-3.** Their colors range from a bright chartreuse to a deep grassy green. Their petite white flowers make them irresistible to bonsai fanciers. Don't be tempted. The roots of both Irish and Scotch moss will penetrate to the bottom of a 5"- deep bonsai pot. **Fig. 3-4.** Once established, these mosses become weeds that will test your persistence. Sometimes the only way to get rid of them is to totally bare-root your bonsai. At first sign of these pesky weeds, get out the tweezers and remove the mosses immediately, being sure to dig deep.

Most weeds, fortunately, are the kind that you might have in your lawn or vegetable garden. These weeds are easily plucked out with tweezers when they're young. **Fig. 3-5.** Larger specimens can still be teased out gently with your hands.

Occasionally a woody seed will find its way to your container by way of the wind, or perhaps in a bird dropping. One of my neighbors has a weeping birch tree she adores. The catkins in the spring start to sprinkle millions of very viable seeds into the breezes, and by June my bonsai are all sprouting tiny birch trees. These "weeds" have long taproots that grow quickly towards the wet bottoms of the pots, where they grow rapidly almost overnight. By the time I see the first few green leaves, the tiny birch is a formidable opponent indeed. By pulling off the top of the plant, I only encourage the roots to hide for one more week. The same "strengthened" birch-tree seedling comes back even faster and more vigorously than it did before. The easiest solution, I have discovered, is to use a popular systemic herbicide. I dip a small watercolor brush into the bottle of herbicide, normally diluted and sprayed, and paint just a bit of it on a green leaf. Since the product is sys-

Fig. 3-1

Fig. 3-2

Fig. 3-3

Fig. 3-4

temic, the poison attacks and kills the long taproot.

When using systemic herbicides, caution is advised. Some trees reproduce by sprouting naturally from hor-

Fig. 3-5

Fig. 3-6

izontal roots. The elm, hawthorn and quince do this routinely. If you choose to paint a herbicide on a particularly persistent weed, make sure it isn't part of your bonsai! **Fig. 3-6.**

Bonsai plants that require frequent watering frequently have weeds. A recently deposited weed seed has a greater chance of getting a nice timely shower after landing on a bonsai that's watered frequently. If you have trouble with common weeds on the soil surface of your juniper or alpine fir, I suspect that you're simply watering your bonsai whether it needs it or not. When I water with a watering can, I water only those plants that need it. When I water with the hose, I tend to water everything just because it's so darned easy! This bad watering habit tends to promote weeds.

A popular ground cover known as baby's tears seems to make its way into bonsai pots. This invasive plant will take over a bonsai planting in just a

few months. Getting rid of it will take just as long. Beware of this innocuous-looking plant!

Just as a good, healthy and compact lawn will resist weeds, a compact moss under your bonsai will help cut down on vegetative pests. I prefer the low type of silvery grey-green moss that grows on stones and concrete. Don't use Irish or Scottish moss, which aren't true mosses. I grind up a bit of the moss between my fingers and sprinkle it on the soil surface. Most of the spores don't survive, but it only takes a few starts to eventually achieve the effect you want. Don't allow moss to cover your whole pot. Too much moss will become a weed in itself.

Two other ground covers that I have found to be superior are called bluestar creeper, **Fig. 3-7,** and linnaria, **Fig. 3-8.** Try locally available ground covers from the garden, forest, or nursery. You may find just the perfect touch under your bonsai and such cover will help fight off weeds, as well.

Fig. 3-7

Fig. 3-8

Chapter 4

SUMMER CARE

Summer presents some unique problems. Regulating the water in a container requires the simultaneous coordination of three main factors. **Fig. 4-1.**

Size of the container. As the width and depth of the container doubles, the volume thus contained increases exponentially. For example, a square pot 1″ (2.5 cm) on a side contains only 1 in.³ (16 cm³) of soil. By contrast, a pot that's 2″ (5 cm) on each side contains 8 in.³ (125 cm³) of soil. Presuming that the first container will dry out in one hour, it's possible that the second, larger container will dry out only after eight hours. The larger pot is the better choice for the working person. Don't be afraid to pot your bonsai in a large pot if you're having difficulty keeping it moist.

Shade probably affects a plant's moisture content more than any other factor. In chapter 12 you'll find that juniper prefers full sunlight all day. If your

bonsai container dries out in four hours, move it to a shadier location. **Fig. 4-2.** This plant needs to be moved before more serious damage occurs. By observing the sun's path across the growing area, you can learn where the "hot spots" are and where the temperature remains naturally cooler. If your juniper still receives morning sun, it will likely still thrive.

Regulate your watering frequency. It may be convenient for you to water both morning and evening, rather than to water only in the morning and have some of your trees suffer all night long. In the summer, insufficient watering is the most serious mistake one can make. **Fig. 4-3.** This maple is unduly stressed by the sun. If your trees dry out daily, there's no problem of overwatering or fungus or rot. Water generously, without concern.

You'll have to make constant adjustments to your watering schedule

Fig. 4-1

Fig. 4-2

Fig. 4-3

depending upon the temperature, humidity, season, location, health of plant, age of tree, degree of pot boundedness, vigor of species, prevailing wind, length of day, altitude, type of planting and styling considerations. Let's consider how each of the above affects our summer care schedule.

Fig. 4-4

Temperature. Every summer there's a local fair here in Oregon that's scheduled sometime in midsummer. It's held in a great open area with musicians on stage, food booths and games for the children. It always rains. I joke with fellow bonsai enthusiasts in the area: If you want to know when to repot your pine, just schedule it during the fair! Sure enough, a few nice cool days precede the downpour and it's perfect summer weather to transplant, repot or defoliate your maples. **Fig. 4-4.** Always use plenty of water when transplanting during the summer. Not all summers are created equal. A few years back, my water bill actually exceeded my electric bill due to unusual demand.

Humidity. A local joke about people in the Northwest says that we don't tan, we rust. Plants feel the humidity, as well as humans. High humidity means that it's difficult to shed excess moisture; for plants that means mildew and fungus (**Fig. 4-5**). When the weather is overcast, warm and muggy, I advise mildew protection for some sensitive species: crab apple, cotoneaster, pyracantha, rose, plum, prune, peach, almond, and pear. A light application of fungicide will protect them from leaf curl, blight, black spot, rust and powdery mildew. It's far easier to target susceptible trees and treat them while they're healthy than it is to wait for them to be infected and try to cure them in a weakened condition.

Seasons. I'm very much aware of the different seasons around the world. My early training in bonsai was from a Japanese book which I read while I lived thousands of miles across the Pacific. I soon discovered that the Japanese seasonal tasks took into account that over there it's dry in the winter and wet in the summer. In Oregon, where I live, it's wet in the winter and dry in the summer. Seasonal adjustments had to be made. In chapter 11, these adjustments have been made by compiling a seasonal checklist.

Location. By location I mean specific location in your growing area, not location in the geographical sense. For example, if you have a nice cool area in your backyard where you like to sit and enjoy your favorite beverage, you might consider this as an excellent place for your Japanese maples. The maples enjoy morning sun, but when the temperature starts to rise in the afternoon, they like to relax under the canopy of a large shade tree with their favorite beverage, water. If, on the other hand, your patio faces south and basks in warm sun every afternoon, you should be able to grow the finest pine and juniper bonsai possible. Some peo-

ple would be green with envy at this opportunity, for their yards are completely shaded with mature trees. Take advantage of your local attributes. Grow what's easiest for you; what's easy for you might be very difficult for another.

Health of plant. A few years back, I was working for a large local nursery wholesaler. I'd volunteered to take care of the container yard for the summer. The automatic watering system wasn't always predictable, and some hand watering was inevitable. The owner arrived unexpectedly one day while I was watering. He said, "I see you're having trouble with the third noble fir from the left." In less than ten seconds, this seasoned nurseryman had spotted root rot in a plant from a distance of 50 yards. Sure enough, three days later the tree was showing severe fungus problems, and ten days later it was dead. Since then, I've honed my observation skills to the point where I can surprise others, just as this skilled nurseryman surprised me. A tree that has a problem will appear different from its neighbors. This difference is actually easier to see from a distance. Close up, one can't accurately compare color to the healthy adjacent plants. The first sign of difficulty is that the stressed tree lacks clarity in color. It's almost as if you were looking through a semitransparent screen surrounding the tree. The green colors fade slightly to grey. The clarity of foliage detail appears out of focus. What's more obvious is that the plant starts using water at a decreased rate, as compared to its close neighbors. When this happens, time is of the essence. A quick shower of systemic fungicide, moving the tree away from the shade and shelter of other plants and restricting water will usually save it. By the time the foliage starts to fall off, it's too late. Be aware of your plant's normal activity. A sudden change in color or a sudden change in water uptake could indicate a serious problem. If you water everything with a sprinkler whether it needs it or not, you'll miss out on an early warning.

Fig. 4-5

Age of tree. Recently transplanted trees should have the protection of full shade for at least ten days. Water these plants every day even though they're not drying out. In two weeks the transplant will start growing vigorously. After this time, apply a low-nitrogen fertilizer to stimulate it further. An actively growing plant should use a tremendous amount of water as it grows. As a bonsai ages, it requires a bit less water and a bit more shade. Let's compare two plants: a five-year-old trident maple bonsai and a fifty-year-old trident maple bonsai. The younger plant can use more fertilizer as it grows to maturity. It will use moisture rapidly as it develops. The five-year-old's moisture consumption will be great in relation to its small size. Its leaves will

be large, and it will tolerate full sun for most of the day. The older maple, of the same variety, will have smaller leaves and will appreciate full shade at two o'clock in the afternoon. Its growth will be slower than the youngster's. The older tree will require less fertilizer and, in spite of it being a grand old tree, its water uptake will be proportionately reduced. Take these factors into consideration when caring for older specimens; they'll appreciate it.

How pot bound? What does "pot bound" mean? I like to think in terms of percentages. If a bonsai container contains half roots and half soil, I call this 50% pot bound. Good bonsai practice allows the percentage of roots to go as high as 90% without causing permanent damage to the bonsai. To be sure, such a plant requires repotting immediately. (See chapter 6.) A bonsai that's 50% pot bound will stay wet longer than a bonsai that's 90% pot bound, although both plants are the same size. By watching a plant's sun and shade tolerance, and observing water uptake, you can predict the root-bound percentage. If a pine tree uses up moisture quickly in spite of being placed in the shade, check its roots. It is probably badly pot bound and could use repotting into a larger container. All summer long, make mental notes of these watering schedules. Irregularities in such schedules could mean that further investigation to determine any problem will be necessary.

Vigor of species. Species such as birch, beech, hornbeam, elm, alder and willow are thirsty plants. **Fig. 4-6.** The elm is a thirsty plant. Water its foliage as well as the pot to help clean off the leaves as well as to provide additional moisture. Mountain and desert conifers use water sparingly, so give them a sunny location and water only when necessary. Avoid watering their foliage. They're not used to such watering in nature.

Fig. 4-6

Prevailing wind. Approaching ground level, wind velocity decreases. The same principle applies regarding trees, fences or houses. If your bonsai is drying out too fast, you may have too much wind. Try moving the bonsai closer to the ground, or tuck it in under the canopy of a tree or the eaves of a house. If a tree has trouble drying out, move it out into the open a bit more, or elevate it on a high shelf. Excessively windy areas may require the construction of a shelter or windbreak. Protect your bonsai on at least two sides in a windy area.

Length of day. As spring progresses towards summer, the sun rises earlier, gains a steep angle towards noon, and then finally sets. The length of the day, the temperature and the steep angle of the sun make for a stressful day for unprotected bonsai. As the days get even longer, you'll find sun on the north side of your home, both in the morning and in the evening. Shade plants left there unprotected can burn easily. The steep angle of the sun severely reduces the amount of shade cast by a tree. Make sure your bonsai benches are protected during hot afternoons.

Altitude. Skiers and mountain climbers know that extra protection from the sun is necessary at higher elevations. Plants also feel the effects of high ultraviolet radiation. In the species checklist (chapter 12), I recommend daylength exposures for the plants listed there. If you live above 3000 ft. (1000 m) in altitude, appropriate adjustments should be made. Above 4000 ft. (1300 m), even greater caution should be taken with plants native to low altitudes. For example, a Japanese maple at sea level will tolerate summer sun from dawn until 1:00 P.M.. At 4000 ft. (1300 m) this same maple must be in full shade by 11:00 A.M. in order to prevent damage.

Type of planting. Perhaps the easiest style of bonsai to care for is the semi-cascade style. It's always planted in a big square pot. It isn't generally very tall, so it won't tip over in a wind gust. The long lower branch doesn't scrape on the bench or hang over the edge of the bench, as does the cascade style. The pot is easy to water and drains well for its size, yet it retains moisture well during hot days. Cascade pots tend to tip over, be it from cats, birds, wind or squirrels. **Fig. 4-7.** The small openings of cascade pots require an extra effort to ensure that adequate moisture reaches the roots. These pots drain exceptionally well. The formal upright style of pot has a tendency to stay wet too long because the wide lower branches shade the surface of the roots. Also, shallow containers don't drain as well as do deep containers. Turn a wet sponge on its end and it will dry out rapidly. Leave it flat and it takes a long time to dry out. The same principle holds true with the shapes of bonsai pots. The most troublesome style of all to care for in summer is the rock planting. **Fig. 4-8.** The small volume of soil plus the increased wind exposure create a constant watering problem. Run a large piece of cord or lantern wick up the back side of your rock planting and fasten it securely in several places to your soil mass with pins or staples. Place the lower end of the wick in a glass of water. The wick will carry water from the glass to the planting by means of capillary action. This is, of course, not suitable for show, but it works for dry summers. **Fig. 4-9.** These small bonsai need water several times a day due to their small containers.

Fig. 4-7

Fig. 4-8

Fig. 4-9

Styling considerations. All styling designs are based on emphasizing the tree's attributes and minimizing the tree's deficiencies. If your tree is weak or underdeveloped, spindly, or has a small trunk, the best favor you can do to promote its style is to pull it from the pot and plant it in the ground for the summer. **Fig. 4-10.** These bonsai are enjoying a fine summer in the ground under a sprinkler. Practise your pot skills on a bonsai that's more highly developed. It makes little sense

Fig. 4-10

to stress a tree, reduce its leaf size, grey its trunk, defoliate it, restrict water, adjust its fertilizer or wire it if its trunk is only as big as a pencil. Plant it in the ground, put a sprinkler on it, and enjoy your summer by going to the beach. When summer is over, the trunk will be significantly larger in size. The tree will be green, healthy and happy. You can then put it back in the bonsai pot and enjoy it during the other three seasons. A well developed bonsai deserves advanced training techniques. An inexpensive, young and partially developed tree could use a vacation in the sun!

Summer's an ideal time to care for the dead wood on your bonsai. Intentional dead tops, branches and strips of grey on the trunk add to the illusion of age. These areas are called *jim, shari* and *saba miki*. In the summer, when it's warm and dry, a light coating of lime sulfur will help keep them a nice color of driftwood-grey, as well as combating insects and disease. Simply dip a small brush into the bottle of liquid lime sulfur and paint the liquid on the dead areas. In warm weather, the initial yellow color will grey out overnight.

Chapter 5

WINTER CARE

Chapters 11 and 12 are closely related to this chapter. The seasonal checklist will suggest timely winter tasks and remind you of seasonal problems to be aware of. The species checklist will give you the minimum temperature for each of your bonsai. Below this temperature, the cold may damage them.

Winter care deals primarily with problems of cold. **Fig. 5-1.** This Chinese elm shows signs of having gotten too cold. There are numerous ways to cope with the problem of cold, and they're as varied as your individual circumstances, your local environment and your garden facilities.

Bonsai owners can protect their trees from excess cold in the following ways: positioning in the yard, burying, mulching, sheltering or heating.

Positioning in the yard. Previously I described how wind decreases under trees, next to a fence, or near the foundation of a house. We're all aware of "wind-chill factor." Plants feel this ef-

fect, as do animals. On a freezing day, plants exposed to wind will suffer, but not the plants that are protected from the wind. Take your bonsai down from their high display shelves in winter, **Fig. 5-2,** and put them on the ground. **Fig. 5-3.** The added protection thus provided is considerable. When temperatures drop below freezing, cluster your bonsai together near the foundation of your home. **Fig. 5-4.** Not only will the wind-chill factor be reduced, but a certain amount of heat leakage from your home, no matter how slight, will also assist your trees. **Fig. 5-5.** A simple cardboard box will help keep the bonsai out of the wind. **Fig. 5-6.** Additional protection may be required from strong directional prevailing winds.

Burying. Just like protection from summer heat, burying or planting your bonsai in the garden protects it from moderate cold. **Fig. 5-7.** If the outside temperature drops to 28°F (−2°C)

Fig. 5-1

Fig. 5-2

Fig. 5-3

Fig. 5-4

Fig. 5-5

Fig. 5-6

Fig. 5-7

for several hours, the soil surface will be frozen, but just 2″ (5 cm) down in the soil, the soil's temperature will remain above freezing. **Fig. 5-8.** Remove the whole plant carefully from the pot. **Fig. 5-9.** If your soil doesn't drain well, just place the bonsai on the soil surface and drag adjacent soil towards the bonsai's root ball. **Fig. 5-10.** If it snows, just push some extra snow towards your tree. Snow's a great insulator. These precautionary measures will provide just enough protection for most outdoor bonsai. (See chapter 11.) Persistent lower temperatures will require

Fig. 5-8

Fig. 5-9

Fig. 5-10

additional protection for your bonsai.

Mulching. First plant your bonsai (without its pot) in a convenient spot out of the wind in your garden. Then push a bunch of freshly fallen leaves up against the tree trunk. If it's deciduous, cover the whole tree, and then sprinkle a bit of granular fertilizer like 16-16-16 over the leaves. **Fig. 5-11.** An amazing thing will happen. The leaves will start to decompose in the presence of the fertilizer and begin to heat up! This is winter protection at its easiest and purest, for this is what

Fig. 5-11

happens in nature. You're recreating this process, just making it more localized and rapid.

Sheltering. In my local climate, the ground will freeze hard for a week each winter, and I must figure out which week it's going to happen. By paying close attention to the evening news and my outside thermometer, I can usually anticipate an unusually severe winter storm. When such a storm happens, I simply bring the most sensitive bonsai into my unheated garage. It's always far warmer in the garage than it is outside, possibly due to heat leakage from the house, the greenhouse effect from the garage windows, or simply because the garage is completely out of the wind. In any case, when the storm is over, the sensitive bonsai can go back outside and seem to suffer no ill effects from their week in partial darkness.

Serious bonsai growers will construct a cold frame for winter protection. This frame consists of a belowground pit with a wooden framework over it. The gaps in the wood can be covered by glass or clear-plastic sheeting. The principle is this: The ground 2′ (0.6 m) below the surface won't freeze solid. The transparent cover will capture the sun's heat and hold it inside the pit. The easiest cold frame to construct is one against the foundation of your home. One of the ventilating holes in the side of the foundation can be incorporated into the pit. Excess heat and/or cold is dispersed through that vent. In the event of bright winter sun, the top is opened slightly to avoid overheating inside. The cold frame should be constructed large enough to be able to hold your entire outdoor bonsai collection. I'm fond of using a cold-frame "framework" above my bonsai bench. **Fig. 5-12.** This structure will support two layers of transparent polyethylene to protect the trees from the cold and wind. If additional heat is required, I use a thermostat. **Fig. 5-13.** This type of thermostat is accurate to 34°F (1°C). I merely plug a small space heater and three light bulbs into the receiving end of the thermostat, place them all under the bench, and cover them with clear plastic. A simple glance from the kitchen window tells me that my bonsai are protected: The light bulbs come on at 34°F (1°C). I use three light bulbs because under those extreme conditions of temperature and humidity, the bulb's life expectancy is short. Your partially outdoor bonsai are already inside your home as houseplants. (See chapter 1.)

For extremely serious bonsai collectors, or for bonsai enthusiasts who live in very harsh winter climates, the best option is to build a heated greenhouse. With the use of automatic thermally controlled shutters, your bonsai area can be kept at a modest 34°F (1°C) at night and allowed to heat up to 48°F (9°C) during the day, a perfect winter for all your outdoor bonsai. Unfortunately, greenhouses can be expensive.

Fig. 5-12

Fig. 5-13

Chapter 6

REPOTTING

Four of the most common bonsai questions are: "Does it need to be repotted?"; "Is it root bound?"; "Is this a good time to repot?" and "Does it need a bigger pot?"

Does it need to be repotted? Bonsai professionals, without a moment of hesitation, will first probe the soil with a fingertip. **Fig. 6-1.** If the soil seems loose and resilient, the answer to this first question will likely be "No, not yet." If the soil resists examination with the fingertip, **Fig. 6-2,** other means of examination will be necessary. Pick up the pot with one hand and gently rock the trunk of the bonsai with the other hand. If the pot is wet and the trunk sways easily when manipulated by hand, the answer will be, "Probably not yet." If the trunk doesn't yield to a rocking motion and the soil appears lightweight and quite compacted, the professional will automatically pull the plant from the pot with one quick, confident jerk. **Fig. 6-**

3. Roots will always congest at the edges of containers; the presence of lots of roots doesn't necessarily mean that the plant is root bound. The professional will gently tease, poke and prod at the root ball that has conformed to the shape of the container, looking for further information. This bonsai, at first glance, appears quite root bound. Further probing reveals that the majority of roots are just on the outside. There's still enough soil inside the root ball to carry this plant through one more season, but it will need to be repotted next year.

This bonsai, **Fig. 6-4,** also appears to be root bound. A fingertip cannot find any soil or traces of resiliency. By grabbing the trunk and pulling gently to and fro, the bonsai is taken slightly out of its container. **Fig. 6-5.** Poking and prodding with the fingertips, there appears to be little soil left within the root ball. Further examination with a root hook, root rake and chopsticks reveals that the soil content in the root

Fig. 6-1

Fig. 6-2

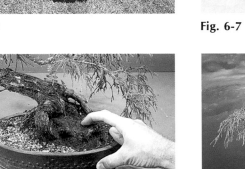

Fig. 6-3

Fig. 6-4

Fig. 6-5

Fig. 6-6

Fig. 6-7

Fig. 6-8

ball has diminished to around 15% by volume. **Fig. 6-6.** Observing the condition of the soil surface, **Fig. 6-7,** the moss isn't healthy. Where a bright green-grey moss would normally thrive, there's a brownish green scum. The root-crowding condition in this pot has forced me to water this bonsai too often. The root ball has demanded this moisture in order for the bonsai to remain healthy, and the high frequency of watering has taken its toll on the surface condition of the soil. This bonsai, seen from a distance, is obviously pot bound. **Fig. 6-8.** The mass of foliage of this bonsai is being supported by a pot that's too small, both visually and biologically. It's time to repot, both for the sake of the bonsai's health and for aesthetics. Pot this tree into a slightly larger container.

First remove all of the scum by using a strong blast of water from the garden hose. **Fig. 6-9.** A toothbrush helps to remove the slippery algae from crevices. Observing the resulting root mass confirms earlier suspicions. The scum was interfering with drainage and, therefore, the health of the bonsai, and also the soil percentage was quite low in the root ball. Notice that the roots remain quite intact, despite the high pressure of the hose.

Once the root ball is clean, comb out the roots. **Fig. 6-10.** There's no need to intentionally rip and tear apart the roots. Some damage is unavoidable, however. Where the roots break apart due to physical force, new roots will sprout and divide into tiny productive root hairs. Use a minimum of force to comb out the roots, keeping them moist at all times. Longer roots don't need to be shortened, since we're

Fig. 6-9

Fig. 6-10

about to repot this bonsai into a larger container, **Fig. 6-11.** The new container is a Japanese drum-style oval brown pot, and its extra 2″ (5 cm) in length will allow for a good visual balance against the extreme slanting style of the trunk.

Cover the drain holes with screen and secure the mesh with wire staples. **Fig. 6-12.** Pour a small quantity of bonsai soil into the bottom of the pot. Apply fresh soil to about 1″ (2.5 cm) in depth. Don't use gravel, chips, or stones in an attempt to improve pot drainage. Using these materials will, in fact, decrease drainage. For best results, make sure that the soil in your pot is homogeneous from top to bottom.

Try the bonsai in the new container. **Fig. 6-13.** Tuck long roots into the pot if they go in easily; otherwise trim them just enough so that they'll fit inside. Position the plant carefully, paying at-

Fig. 6-11

Fig. 6-15

Fig. 6-12

Fig. 6-16

Fig. 6-13

Fig. 6-17

Fig. 6-14

Fig. 6-18

tention to surface height of the exposed roots, slant of the trunk, and how the tree looks from the back and sides.

Slowly add fresh bonsai soil to the top of the root ball. **Fig. 6-14.** Don't press the soil down with your fingertips, because all you'll accomplish is to compress the root ball below the soil. Use a pair of chopsticks instead, and continually vibrate and thrust new soil particles into and around the roots. **Fig. 6-15.** To do a satisfactory job, this process should take about ten minutes. After you've added as much soil as you can, with your fingertips form a small soil depression around the inside rim of the pot. **Fig. 6-16.** This depression will improve the appearance of the planting, and will make it easier to water without flooding soil over the edge of the pot.

Finish the soil surface with a one-inch-(2.5 cm)wide soft brush. **Fig. 6-17.** There are small bonsai whisks made for this purpose, but I find that an angled finishing brush does the best job.

The completed planting. **Fig. 6-18.** Compare it to **Fig. 6-8.** The larger container nicely balances the extreme slant of the trunk. The container drains really well, now that the congested roots are combed out and the unsightly algae scum has been scrubbed away.

The addition of moss to the soil surface can be accomplished easily by placing small plugs of moss that have been taken from the garden. Sidewalk moss or moss that's growing on old brick is best. Avoid using the large, rangy mosses that grow on trees. **Fig. 6-19.** Not only is it difficult to capture

and remove the roots, but if transplanted successfully, this type of moss grows coarse and tall, and is inappropriate for bonsai. When gathering moss from the ground, **Fig. 6-20,** make sure that the source is weed-free, dense and compact, and will grow in the sun. This sample is leggy, sparse, full of weed seeds and growing in the shade. Again, an inappropriate choice for transfer to a bonsai pot.

Repotting a bonsai from a small pot to an even smaller pot is sometimes necessary and desirable. This rhododendron bonsai is good, but a bit ordinary. **Fig. 6-21.** The trunk is the main deficiency in this design. Not only is the trunk size small for bonsai purposes, it also lacks character, definition and a well-defined root buttress. **Fig. 6-22.** On the back side, however, we can see a bit more trunk strength,

Fig. 6-19

Fig. 6-20

Fig. 6-21

Fig. 6-25

Fig. 6-22

Fig. 6-26

Fig. 6-23

Fig. 6-27

Fig. 6-24

Fig. 6-28

Fig. 6-29

Fig. 6-30

exposed roots and taper. **Fig. 6-23.** Unfortunately, because of the appearance of the upper branches and foliage, this is the *back* of the tree.

Here's the solution: Use the trunk as the strong point of this bonsai. Eliminate the defects by pruning away the foliage and start all over again with a new, clearer style. Instead of a bushy, ordinary plant, redesign this bonsai into a striking miniature bonsai by severely pruning off the lengthy branches. **Fig. 6-24.** With some pruning, we can start to appreciate this trunk line. **Fig. 6-25.** With still further pruning, we can start to imagine the future container for this rhododendron. It will need a container the size of the green Japanese bonsai pot shown in **Fig. 6-26.** How can we possibly get such a large plant into such a small container?

Comb out the roots as you did before, using a root hook, chopsticks, and a root rake. A radically bent dinner fork will work well also. Remove large roots and retain carefully all the close-in small roots near the trunk. **Fig. 6-27.** Try the root ball in the new container. Remove the roots that impede repotting. Keep the roots moist at all times. When the plant finally fits the pot in the position you desire, add a bit of compost back into the container and carefully work it around the sparse remaining roots with chopsticks, as before. **Fig. 6-28.**

When enough bonsai soil has been incorporated into the root ball, pack the surface edge down with your fingertips to form a tidy mound that complements the exposed roots. Form a small landscape hill by planting the miniature bonsai high in the pot. **Fig. 6-29.** This method of planting considerably increases the volume of soil in the pot.

One year later, the new miniature bonsai is a striking tree. **Fig. 6-30.** A mediocre bonsai can rise to be a superior bonsai just by moving it to a smaller container and pruning it back severely. Compare this bonsai to **Fig. 6-21.** The trunk now appears larger and more dominant, and displays attractive surface rootage. The former "bushy" appearance has been refined into one simple trunk line. Repotting can accomplish aesthetic purposes, as well as provide for the continued health of the bonsai.

Repotting can intensify a design, as well. This simple landscape design, **Fig. 6-31,** is understated. Three small cypresses, *Chamaecyparis thyoides andelyensis conica,* stand lonely in a small container with a single lava cave rock. By adding additional rocks and trees,

Fig. 6-31

Fig. 6-32

Fig. 6-33

this simple statement can be made stronger. **Fig. 6-32.** Repotting these three trees into a larger container and adding twenty more trees just like them makes a strong design statement, and makes it easier to care for this miniature landscape. **Fig. 6-33.** Because of the increased volume of soil, this larger planting will need water only once every two days in the summer. The smaller, previous landscape would dry out in about four hours. Repotting into a larger container can considerably reduce maintenance.

You've now repotted into a larger container, both for the health of the plant and to improve design. You've repotted into a smaller container for improved design only. The lesson is this: If, for design purposes, it becomes attractive to repot a bonsai into a smaller container, then so be it. That decision is valid. If you desire lower maintenance and a higher expectation of survival of your bonsai, repot into a larger container. Better to have a live bonsai in a slightly overpotted condition than to have a dead tree in the "perfect" pot.

Chapter 7

INSECTS

The number and variety of insects on our planet is incomprehensible. Fortunately for bonsai growers, relatively few of this vast array pose a threat. Even among those insects that are found on our trees, some are quite beneficial, rather than harmful. For example, this beetle making its way across the moss under a bonsai elm is just passing through. **Fig. 7-1.** There's no need to panic. it's just looking for organic debris and motionless insects to feed upon.

I used to do a radio program where listeners would call the station with their gardening problems. I'd answer their questions live on the air and suggest solutions for their concerns and difficulties. It was interesting to most listeners that problems with insects could be solved over the radio without me ever actually laying eyes on the offending pest. This was possible because nature tends to clump its creatures into functional groups. As one alert listener

remarked, "The only people who care to know the exact identification of an insect are entomologists and fly fishermen!" Let's look at the functional groupings of insects and discuss some ways to control them.

SOFT-BODIED, SUCKING INSECTS

This huge insect classification includes the ever-present aphid, white fly, **Fig. 7-2,** thrip, mite and mealybug. These insects are mobile only when they have to be. They prefer staying in one general area, sucking the sap of the tree and depositing their waste, known as honeydew. They all proliferate at an astounding rate, their generation time measured in hours, not days. One aphid today means twenty aphids tomorrow, so carefully observe your plants. Fortunately, the eradication of these pests is easy. Slowly mix one-half

Fig. 7-1

Fig. 7-2

youngsters after being sprayed the first time. The reason most "organic" sprays don't work is the lack of the applicator's persistence. You have to be willing to exceed the insects' tenacity with careful observation and repeated applications. Don't be tempted to increase the soap concentration or overwet the plant. These measures will only endanger the plant, not the insects.

CATERPILLARS

The signs of damage from caterpillars are unmistakable. **Fig. 7-3.** Large crescent-shaped areas are missing from the edges of leaves. The caterpillar usually avoids the midrib and major veins of leaves because they're too tough to eat. Encasing itself in a rolled-up leaf with its web around it, this voracious eater may rest for the hottest part of the day, preferring to munch away at night.

teaspoon (2.5 ml) of liquid dish detergent into one quart (one litre) of water in a hand-held spray bottle. There's no need to use a compressed air–type applicator. Don't shake the solution, or excess foam will interfere with the siphoning action of the inner tube.

Apply this spray at dusk when the wind and temperature are down. Wet the upper and lower surfaces of the foliage to the point where the liquid begins to drip. Especially spray into cracks, knotholes and surface irregularities in the bark where insects can hide at night. Reapply this solution every three days for a minimum of two weeks. Don't depend on a single application to remove all the pests. Future generations of insects are already in egg form and waiting to hatch. An aphid can switch to "Plan B" under the stress of insecticides, and can actually give birth to hundreds of live

Fig. 7-3

The best way to eradicate these pests is to go out after sundown, armed with a flashlight and a pair of tweezers. Even large amounts of damage can be due to only one caterpillar. There's no need to mix toxic sprays and treat your whole bonsai collection. Just go out, find that bug and squash it! For the squeamish, sometimes it helps to look at your damaged leaves first in order to get up your nerve to do this nasty deed. If your surrounding trees are loaded with caterpillars, you might have to seek professional eradication because of the danger of reinfesting your bonsai.

SPIDERS

This common garden inhabitant is only trying to catch flying insects. It's not eating your bonsai! **Fig. 7-4.** Spider webs are unsightly and certainly should be removed from a bonsai before a show. There's nothing quite like the exhilarating experience of running face-first into an invisible web early in the morning in your garden. Excess webbing can be torn down, although most webs will be rebuilt in just a few hours. I try to keep down the number of flying insects in my garden by clearing up wet debris, by not watering in the evening, and by draining off any standing water. Don't leave empty buckets or containers outside that can accumulate even minute amounts of water. These containers can become insect watering holes and hatcheries

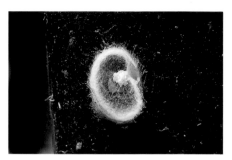

Fig. 7-5

for mosquito larvae. Spiders will build webs where the food is plentiful. Take care of the flying insects and the spiders will dine elsewhere. If you happen across a spider's nest where thousands of tiny spiders are hatching, just physically remove the nest. **Fig. 7-5.**

PROTECTED PESTS

Good examples of this category include the spittle bug, scale insects and the woolly aphid. These insects all surround themselves with a protective coating or growth. The spittlebug's bubbly film is easily washed away with a forceful stream of soapy water. The scale insect protects itself with a hard crust over itself. The soft-bodied insect inside this crust is highly vulnerable to any insecticide. Simply cover their outside coating with a heavy layer of mineral oil delivered on the tip of a cotton swab. **Fig. 7-6.** This oily layer will suffocate the scale inhabitant. The woolly aphid protects itself with a cottonlike substance that it secretes. The minute fibres repel water and, therefore, insecticides as well. A product known to orchard farmers as "spreader-sticker" is the solution to this problem. This product is a wetting agent and oil-based sticky substance combined. Sim-

Fig. 7-4

Fig. 7-6

Fig. 7-7

ple detergent plus this sticker-spreader will penetrate the previously unwettable surface of the "wool," thereby eliminating the now-susceptible pest.

BORING INSECTS

If you see a hole about the size of a nail shank in your tree, you probably have a boring insect inside. Even some antique furniture, hundreds of years old, has this problem. The insect drills a small access hole into the wood, and then spends the rest of its life safely tucked away inside the heartwood of your valued bonsai. On deadwood, the borer produces a small hole. Underneath live bark, the borer stimulates a constantly festering ooze of sap as the tree tries to protect itself from this rude invasion. **Fig. 7-7.** Where the entrance hole is visible, use a syringe to inject any insecticide directly into the opening. When the hole is obscured by the constant flow of sap, a treatment of the whole plant is necessary with a systemic insecticide. Follow the directions on the label, except apply to bonsai only half the recommended dose. Better to be forced to apply a second time than to have the first application damage your tree. This damage, **Fig. 7-8,** is due to a copper-wire loop that was

Fig. 7-8

forgotten at the base of this pine tree. Notice the similar appearance to **Fig. 7-7.** The tree is just trying to protect itself from invasion by a foreign host, whether it be from a boring insect or from a forgotten copper wire loop.

SLUGS & SNAILS

These garden pests are omnipresent. Snails, prized by some as *escargots*, are quite repulsive to others. **Fig. 7-9.** The damage they do occurs mainly at night, when their sticky, slimy bodies can move across surfaces with ease. In the morning, look for the whitish trails of slime that they leave behind. Damage to foliage is random, sometimes just at the edge of a leaf (as a caterpillar might do) but the powerful mouths of slugs and snails can create great holes in the middle of a leaf as well. These slow-moving creatures can usually be found lurking in the shade or moist bottom surface of a plant's container. Notice the culprit caught on the shady side of this pot.

Both snails and slugs have a fondness for beer, which is their downfall. Buy the least expensive brew you can find; these pests don't exhibit good taste in beer. Pour about an inch of beer into an empty tuna can and place the can near the problem area. In the morning, the snail's party will be over, and there's nothing but the mess to clean up.

Fig. 7-10

Fig. 7-9

age patterns are quite noticeable and characteristic, however. **Fig. 7-10.** Small notches taken from the outer borders of leaves are well rounded and accompanied by a narrow brown, dry border. Damage is never so complete that it totally destroys a whole leaf, as a caterpillar might do. Characteristically, the weevil primarily attacks the lower leaves only, because it would be too difficult to climb from the soil at sundown, travel to the top of the tree and still get back into its hiding place in the soil by sunrise. A caterpillar would just as soon attack the succulent new growth at the top of the tree and roll up into a convenient leaf for a daytime nap.

Granular insecticides deter these soil pests. They're easily applied, like salt to an icy sidewalk. A light, even application is sufficient. Cover the granules with a layer of compost to make them more efficient. For persistent cases, an application of systemic insecticide may be necessary.

WEEVILS

Just when you thought it was easy to eradicate garden pests, along comes the weevil and its close relatives. These insects are never seen. Even at night they're hard to see or catch. Their dam-

GALL APHIDS

These insects are perhaps the most persistent pests known to bonsai. Fortunately, they aren't common, and since they're limited to high-altitude conifers, their importance is considerably diminished. The insect burrows into the newly forming buds of spruce, fir, hemlock, pine and juniper. The infected bud tries to expand and grow, but cannot, because this parasite is nesting inside it. **Fig. 7-11.** These new buds of Western silver fir are swelled up and deformed, and the needles seem embedded in the bark. Once the gall has formed, it means that the damage has been done. The insect has gone to another location on the tree to attack fresh buds. The only good solution for gall is to apply systemic insecticide in late winter/early spring. I've tried for years to cut out the infected parts with a pruning tool, only to be disappointed the following year by the emergence of new infection sites. Apply the systemic solution starting in late winter, before bud growth begins. Three light applications two weeks apart are far more effective than one full-strength application. Protect the bonsai roots from runoff from the foliage. After four hours, rinse the entire bonsai off with a gentle spray of clear water.

The following "pests" really aren't problems at all.

This simple moth, **Fig. 7-12,** isn't eating your bonsai. It's a nocturnal creature and is parked here only temporarily. When evening comes, it'll be gone.

These resin flecks are normal for a bristlecone pine, *Pinus aristata.* **Fig. 7-13.** These flecks look similar to scale insects and, indeed, on any other pine they'd be quite alarming to see. Even the most experienced nurserymen may confuse the two.

This rhododendron is exhibiting its fall color. **Fig. 7-14.** Three-year-old leaves will always change color in August and September. This change is quite normal, and although this color is brownish and unattractive, it doesn't indicate an insect infestation. Count back from this year's growth on the end of the branch. The second year's growth should be green, mature and well hardened off. In August, the third-year growth will change color before falling off by November. All broadleaf evergreens exhibit this color change and shedding.

The word *evergreen* is a bit of a misnomer. All that this term really means is that every year, one whole year of foliage growth will fall off the tree. In the case of deciduous trees, the growth that falls off is one year old. In the case of evergreens, the leaves or needles that fall off are all three years old. Look at a 4000-year-old bristlecone pine; there are no 4000-year-old needles on it; the needles drop off when they're three years old. **Fig. 7-15.** This pine, is shown in late summer; its three-year-old needles are starting to turn yellow. This coloration isn't due to insect damage; it's natural.

Fig. 7-11

Fig. 7-12

Fig. 7-13

Fig. 7-14

This rhododendron isn't being attacked by insects or disease. **Fig. 7-16.** Its location is too windy. The damage shown on this leaf is due to nothing but physical forces. There's no need to get out the insecticide or the fungicide. Notice particularly the pattern of damage. Insects always make wide curving or round holes in leaves, and they avoid the leaf's veins. The damage shown cuts *across* the veins. This distinction defines mechanical damage versus insect damage.

The yellow growth found on this alpine fir is typical of the shock these high-altitude plants go through when they try to adjust to low altitudes. **Fig. 7-17.** This yellowing is a normal transition, and the plan will recover nicely. The shock that this tree is feeling is normal, considering the major change that's occurring to its physiology. The worst thing that you can do at this

Fig. 7-15

Fig. 7-16

Fig. 7-17

Fig. 7-18

point is to assume that the plant is suffering from insect damage or lack of fertilizer. An application of either insecticide or fertilizer could be the last straw for this suffering plant. Water deeply when dry, but don't overwater, spray or fertilize this plant; it'll be fine in one year's time.

In midsummer, particularly when it gets very hot, new growth will sometimes come out as small reddish brown shoots. This English oak bonsai, *Quercus robur*, normally has chartreuse new growth. When the thermometer gets above 100°F (37.8°C) the new shoots appear brownish red. **Fig. 7-18.** This coloration is natural. We see leaves as green because the red end of the sun's color spectrum is absorbed by the leaf. We see the green spectrum, which is being reflected off the leaf and is picked up by our eyes. When new leaves in the summer appear red, it's only because they're absorbing light at the cool (green) end of the sun's spectrum. The hot end of the spectrum (the red end) is rejected and is reflected towards our eyes. The plant is merely trying to protect its new growth from ultraviolet rays. Such coloration is a plant's way of providing its own "sunblock." This sudden seasonal change in color is due neither to insects nor disease; the change is a natural function of a

healthy plant trying to make its way through a difficult season.

Let me now reinforce two important points. Most insects are highly overrated as pests. Good observation and judicious application of common detergent will normally suffice to take care of the occasional insect problem. There's much that you can do to create a healthy environment for your trees. Water in the morning, remove standing water, and water only as needed. Encourage the presence of natural insect predators in your garden by cutting back on pesticides except when absolutely necessary. Let's share our natural world with helpful insects: praying mantis, ladybug, dragonfly, and spider. **Fig. 7-19.** Lizards are valuable for insect control, as well.

Fig. 7-19

Chapter 8

DISEASES

In the plant world, *disease* refers to the natural process by which the cellulose of living tissues is recycled back into compost. In the case of bonsai, we'd like to slow down that process. We'd prefer not to see our favorite pine-tree bonsai turn into compost. **Fig. 8-1.** Yet, this natural force is always present and at work in nature, twenty-four hours a day. The task of the bonsai grower is to slow down this process so that he can enjoy watching his trees grow and develop. Without this "interference," bonsai will naturally wither, decline, rot and return to the earth.

Let's look at the way compost is made. Leaves, twigs and dead roots in the presence of moisture and certain microorganisms quickly decay into humus. By turning over such material, and incorporating nitrogen and oxygen as well as more moisture, we can accelerate the process considerably.

Thinking in reverse, can we slow down this process? We can limit nitrogen, moisture and dead leaves and twigs. There are, of course, fungicides to assist the grower, but there's nothing as powerful as prevention.

The bonsai should be kept clean of falling leaves, seed casings or other debris. Immediately prune off dead twigs, spent flower petals and loose bark. Treat all "driftwood" areas with lime sulfur, straight from the bottle. This juniper trunk is starting to get soft and green because of excess moisture. **Fig. 8-2.** This area should be scrubbed clean with a toothbrush, then preserved with lime sulfur applied full-strength with a small brush. **Fig. 8-3.** This driftwood area on a bonsai juniper is healthy. **Fig. 8-4.** Notice the bright grey color. The trunk is dry, sun-bleached, and treated with lime sulfur to help preserve its excellent condition.

This is the bark of a bonsai oak tree. **Fig. 8-5.** Since this is live bark, and not an intentional dead area on a bonsai, keep it clean, but not as bright a color as driftwood-grey. Apply a dilute mixture of lime sulfur (instead of full-strength). I recommend about one tablespoon (15 ml) per quart (litre) of water. Scrub the trunk with a toothbrush that's been slightly moistened in this solution. The trunk won't turn its full grey color for forty-eight hours, so don't judge the color immediately. If you want a lighter color on the trunk, just reapply some more solution. The mixture will keep its strength for several weeks.

Fig. 8-1

Fig. 8-2

Fig. 8-3

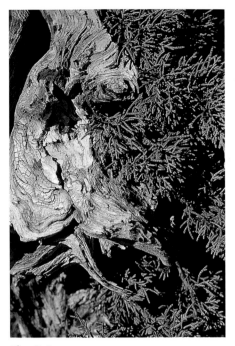
Fig. 8-4

The bonsai bench should be made of cedar or redwood; these woods naturally resist decay. Or, construct a bench surface of hardware cloth or soffit screen stretched across a lumber framework. Move the bonsai around often and once a week wash off the bench under each pot, since disease organisms will hide there. Once a year, in summer, remove all your bonsai from the bench and apply a strong bleach solution to the entire bench, its legs, cross supports, back, and especially the surface. I like to apply a solution of half water and half household bleach to my bench using a hand-pressurized insecticide sprayer. Scrub away green scum with a stiff brush. Leave the solution on for an hour, hose it off with fresh water and return the bonsai to their places again. If you prefer the bench to have a natural brown wood color, rather than a bleached appearance, apply a wood preservative to the bench one week later. Give the bleach time to work.

If possible, try not to water the trunks of your trees. I realize it's easier to broadcast a spray of water from the end of a hose than it is to water with a watering can, but constant moisture on the bark creates the scum shown in **Figs. 8-1** and **8-5.** Try to lower the water pressure on your hose so that you can duplicate the stream of water that comes from the end of a bonsai watering can. Refer to **Fig. 2-7.** This pine tree is still watered well while the trunk and foliage stay dry.

If algae start to form on the surface of your pot, it's because the roots are too crowded, you've applied too much fertilizer, or you're watering too much. **Fig. 8-6.** Sometimes all three errors exist, as in this case. The solution to this problem is a firm blast from the garden hose and some scrubbing with a toothbrush. This clean soil surface, **Fig. 8-7,** now drains well and the bonsai is ready for repotting into a larger container.

Try to water in the morning, rather than later. You'll be watering in the morning dew, before it has a chance to evaporate, adding sufficient additional moisture to last through the heat of the day. Avoid watering at night because the bonsai will take too long to dry off. Both insects and disease enjoy this prolonged wet condition; slugs love it too. If your bonsai requires water twice a day, the second watering should be about one hour before sundown. The bonsai will get a chance to dry out before nightfall. Wet foliage attracts fungus spores; they stick to wet surfaces better than to dry surfaces. Most common moulds and mildews are

Fig. 8-5

Fig. 8-6

Fig. 8-7

aided by excess water or by watering at the wrong time of the day, such as this rust, **Fig. 8-8,** this powdery mildew, **Fig. 8-9,** and this black spot, **Fig. 8-10.** Fungicides, of course, will treat these problems, but so will proper watering.

A lesser-known disease is called "shot hole," **Fig. 8-11,** for obvious reasons. Most people wouldn't recognize this as a fungus problem. The holes in the leaves make one think that an insect is responsible for the damage, but this isn't the case. This fungal dis-

Fig. 8-8

Fig. 8-9

Fig. 8-10

Fig. 8-11

ease prefers elm, hornbeam, alder, birch, beech, and zelkova. Fungal spores in damp climates attach to the undersides of the leaves and rot away a small hole in the leaf. The presence of small, brownish, half-rotted spots sometimes helps to identify this as a fungus rather than insect damage. The only success I've had, once I find this damage on my bonsai, is an application at dusk of a powdered systemic fungicide. Follow the application instructions found on the product label.

Another problem caused by overwatering is root rot. **Fig. 8-12.** These four pine trees were intentionally overwatered for three weeks in midsummer heat. Sure enough, I was able to kill two of them, with just water! The tree on the left still has no signs of disease. The tree next to it is just starting to get the characteristic cloudy grey color in the foliage. At this point, this tree can be saved by washing all the soil off the roots, trimming away the slippery black dead roots, immersing the entire plant in fungicide and repotting into fresh soil. The third tree from the left is already too far gone; it can't be saved. The fourth tree is already dead. The first two trees were saved by early detection, but I hope you can see how subtle this disease is. Water a plant when *it* needs it, not when *you* need to water, and most of your disease problems will be solved.

Fig. 8-12

Fig. 8-13

Fig. 8-14

Fig. 8-15

There are three conditions that aren't really diseases at all. This broadleaf evergreen is often thought to be diseased, **Fig. 8-13.** Actually, this plant is just a variety of *Aucuba*, which has a mottled or variegated leaf. Some people like this variety, some don't, but it's definitely not diseased. This same shrub, however, is sensitive to sunlight, and when it's planted in a sunny location takes on this diseased appearance. **Fig. 8-14.** This plant isn't diseased, it just looks terrible. Change its location to the shade, trim off all the sunburned leaves and you'll have a healthy plant. When a plant is stressed like this one, don't spray it with a pesticide.

The mossy growth on this pine tree is quite natural and isn't a disease of any kind. **Fig. 8-15.** This growth, *lichens*, can be removed easily with a brush, if desired. This removal is just a question of personal aesthetics. Some prefer only the grey growth and remove the orange growth. Some remove it all. Still others think that this type of growth gives their bonsai a nice "natural" appearance. This growth is an indicator of good air quality; lichens are not found on urban trees in densely populated areas. In any case, lichens aren't harmful. Keep them or remove them as you wish; they're not disease organisms.

Chapter 9

BONSAI SOILS & FERTILIZERS

By the turn of the last century, many bonsai exhibits started appearing all over Europe and the United States. Paris saw its first major bonsai exhibit during the same World's Fair for which the Eiffel Tower was built. Great Britain hosted several major bonsai exhibitions between 1900 and 1910. New York, San Francisco, and Chicago had already seen their first examples of this Asian art form.

Because these trees failed to thrive under the care of Westerners, it was assumed that there was some Asian secret to keeping an old tree alive in a small container. If there was a "secret" to keeping bonsai alive, it certainly can be revealed now. The "average" bag of potting soil contains material that's so harmful that you couldn't possibly keep a bonsai alive in it for more than eighteen months.

The harmful components of most potting soils aren't the materials themselves, but the *size* of these materials. Clay won't support plant life because its particles are too small. Similarly, gravel doesn't make a good potting soil because its particles are too large. These Japanese-made stainless-steel screens are made for creating bonsai soil, **Fig. 9-1.** The large round hoops hold a variety of interchangeable screens, **Fig. 9-2.**

Making bonsai soil is simple. Remove all the smallest particles; they interfere with drainage, block the flow of oxygen and carbon dioxide, and they decompose too rapidly. Also, remove all the *largest* particles; they're inefficient because they use up too much valuable room in a bonsai pot. Good bonsai soil is, therefore, just ordinary soil that's been screened twice: once to remove the small dust and powder, the second time to remove the large, inef-

Fig. 9-1

Fig. 9-3

Fig. 9-2

ficient chunks. This screening process is labor-intensive, but the results are spectacular. Suddenly your bonsai will thrive under even the most stressful conditions! Take the time and effort to prepare your soil and you'll be rewarded many times over by the fantastic results. Bonsai soil is the perfect potting soil. Once you've tried it and seen its success, you'll never buy another bag of commercial "potting soil."

Start with any good soil from your garden or from a bag from a plant nursery. Dry the soil sufficiently so that it can be easily screened (wet or soggy soil clumps together). Discard any particles that will pass through common window screen. Buy bonsai soil screens or staple window screen to the bottom of a wooden box. Throw away any particle that will *not* pass through ⅛″ (0.3 cm) soffit screen (also called "hardware cloth"). Bravo! You've just made bonsai soil! **Fig. 9-3.**

I find that conifers prefer soils made primarily of rock, sand, gravel, perlite, mica, vermiculite, cat litter, or other mineral products. Azaleas, rhododendrons, indoor bonsai and broad-leafed evergreens seem to thrive in old sawdust, bark, leaf litter, compost, sphagnum or similar organic materials. Fruiting and flowering trees enjoy a good balance between these two extremes. For a more detailed soil discussion, I refer you to the chapter on soil in *The Bonsai Workshop* (Sterling Publishing Co., Inc., 1994).

FERTILIZER

There's much discussion these days about the source of fertilizer and its effect on plants. Some say that nitrogen from fish, for example, is better than nitrogen from ammonia or urea. I believe that there's no fertilizer made that will supply all the nutritional needs of your bonsai. Let me explain.

Suppose you're raising a puppy or a kitten. You go to the grocery store and pick out a brand of pet food that you like. For the rest of its life, that dog or that cat is going to get that food, and no other food. No scraps from the table, no treats for being good. Can you be assured that the product you selected would satisfy every nutritional need that your pet might have for its entire life? Of course not.

Similarly, plant food is best when it comes from a variety of sources. I'm a biochemist. I'm not convinced that two fertilizers, both labelled 5-10-10, are identical, one from urea, the other from fish sources. The other trace minerals and salts that accompany this basic combination of nitrogen, phosphorus and potassium make these two similarly labelled fertilizers quite different indeed. You'll find that the seasonal and species checklists in chapters 11 and 12 will be helpful to this discussion of fertilizers.

Every fertilizer is required to display its NPK rating prominently on its packaging. For example, the numbers 6-4-5 indicate that the product contains 6% nitrogen, 4% phosphorus, and 5% potassium.

Nitrogen is perhaps the most important plant nutrient. It provides the lush green growth associated with healthy plants. Nitrogen isn't a mineral, it's a gas. It must be trapped along with other compounds or trapped by nitrogen-capturing bacteria or trapped by other plants (some legumes, for example) in order to be utilized by the plant. Many plant enzymes, proteins and, of course, chlorophyll depend heavily on the supply of nitrogen in the soil. Clover captures nitrogen from the atmosphere. Bonsai cannot. This zelkova leaf shows obvious signs of nitrogen deprivation. **Fig. 9-4.** Notice especially where the yellowing first occurs—away from the veins of the leaves. These signs of yellowing can be observed in conifers as well. Use a magnifying glass on the underside of a pine

Fig. 9-4

needle and you can observe the same phenomenon. Excess nitrogen creates excess growth. This isn't something you want in your bonsai. Watch for the first signs of yellowing and apply a well-balanced fertilizer. Don't wait for this degree of yellowing before applying fertilizer.

Phosphorus particles are mineral, and they don't dissolve like nitrogen. Phosphorus in liquid fertilizers is only in the bottle because it was put there by the manufacturer. Unless you shake the bottle well, it hides down at the bottom somewhere, reluctant to come out. Phosphorus deficiency can be seen as poor bud development and spindly growth. Phosphorus must be replenished often in container soil because this mineral in the existing soil is depleted quickly as new roots extract it during growth.

Potassium, another mineral, is the third element found in fertilizer. It's consumed at nearly the same rate as nitrogen and is important for ion exchange between the root hairs and the soil particles. Large amounts of potassium are necessary in container soils because only a small percentage of it is useful to the plant. Potassium deficiency can be observed as poor flower color, wilting, and few nuts or berries.

Probably the best bonsai fertilizer

Fig. 9-5

Fig. 9-6

simple watering can. **Fig. 9-5.** First, put three or four drops of liquid fertilizer into the can. The force of filling the can from the faucet mixes the fertilizer well. Then simply pour the water on the bonsai soil. This type of spout never clogs up, as do the spouts on more expensive cans.

When I have to fertilize a number of potted plants, **Fig. 9-6,** I find this siphoning device useful. **Fig. 9-7.** The brass fitting goes between the faucet and the watering hose. The rubber tube drops down into a bucket of water. Mix the granular or liquid fertilizer in the bucket and then water your plants with the hose. Diluted fertilizer is siphoned up into the hose and you can water and fertilize your plants safely, without causing a chemical "burn."

Caution is advised with some fertilizers. I seem to attract the neighborhood cats when I use fish-based fertilizers. Blood meal, used sparingly, seems to deter deer, however. Bonemeal and hoof and horn products seem to fascinate the squirrels and birds, so I avoid using them. Products that advertise time release by "osmosis" I avoid for bonsai purposes. These are temperature-sensitive products, and they can't be used in early spring or late fall.

formula would be one with a 5-10-10 rating that was made from organic sources and had trace minerals added along with iron, calcium, magnesium, sulfur, zinc, and manganese. I've never seen such a product. What I've found is a variety of fertilizers, such as 10-15-10, 3-10-10, 5-10-5, and 1-2-1. These fertilizers are all fine, but I'd recommend changing brands and types from time to time.

I particularly like liquid concentrated fertilizers. They're easy to dissolve, apply, and clean up. Granular products tend to cake up over time on the shelf, and they tend to clog spray applicators. Time-release capsules are fine if they're mixed in with the soil during repotting. Granular fertilizers dumped on the soil surface will form scum and liverwort, and contribute to fungus disease. **Refer to Fig. 3-2.** I can't recommend them. My favorite fertilizer applicator for bonsai is this

Fig. 9-7

Apply fertilizers only after watering. Wait an hour and then water again to prevent green algae from forming. Don't spray liquid fertilizer all over everything everywhere. Tree trunks will become green, the bonsai bench will get slippery, and you'll encourage weeds all over your growing area. Apply fertilizer sparingly, and only to the bonsai soil itself. I recommend a few drops of 5% nitrogen, such as 5-10-5, in a gallon (4 litres) of water to be applied to all bonsai every ten days from February through October.

Vary your fertilizers regularly. Mix in a bit of bonemeal once in a while, or Epsom salts once a year. Most important, observe your bonsai carefully. If its leaves begin to look like those shown in **Fig. 9-4,** you've waited two months too long!

Chapter 10

EMERGENCY TREATMENT

INSPECTION

A bonsai can show many kinds of stress. Sometimes this stress comes from a single source. Other times, it may be due to a variety of insults. Observe your tree thoroughly from top to bottom. Look for subtle signs of stress. Examine the foliage. If it's damaged, specifically where is it damaged? What do the undersides of the leaves look like? If the foliage is wilted, is the root ball dry or wet? Is there a change in color normal for the plant? Are the woody branches affected in any way? Are portions of the trunk discolored or soft? Do the surface roots seem slippery?

Gently pull the plant from the pot and inspect the root ball. Start by smelling the root mass. Does it smell like mushrooms or rotting vegetables? Is the soil completely, or almost, ab-

sent? Are the root hairs white and crisp? Do you see dark, slippery roots? Are fungus or mycorrhizae present? Examine the empty pot. Do you find any insects, excess calcified scale or large cracks?

Inspect as thoroughly as possible. Too often, wilting is seen only as lack of water. The bonsai will be watered and then ignored. A wilted plant may be trying to signal a more profound problem. Use your powers of observation carefully. Sometimes it's not just your eyes that will discover the damage. Use your nose and your touch, as well. Manipulate the branches and the trunk carefully; you may discover an invisible mechanical break caused by a fall or a squirrel. Squeeze and poke at the roots with a finger and smell the freshly opened-up soil for signs of root rot.

Spend several minutes going over every surface of your bonsai. The correct identification of a problem often is the result of combining two seemingly unrelated problems. Sometimes your plant has more than one problem.

When you're confident that you've carefully gone over every square inch of your bonsai, proceed down the following checklist for emergency care. You may have to refer back to your bonsai to double-check your observations. If, after completely going through the following list, you're still unsure of the correct identification and treatment of your tree's problem, you'll find a "generic" solution at the end of this chapter.

Observation	Possible Cause	Suggested Treatment
Wilted foliage, dry root ball	Not enough water	Soak bonsai root ball, pot and all, in a shallow tray, such as a cat-litter box. Place in full shade and mist the foliage.
Persistent wilted foliage, dry root ball	Root bound	Repot immediately. Spray foliage with an antidesiccant such as Wilt-Pruf. Trim roots carefully and place plant in a larger container, if necessary.
Wilted foliage, wet root ball, smelly roots	Root rot	Remove plant from container and clean roots with the force of the hose nozzle. Trim away all dark, slippery roots. Immerse roots in a solution of systemic fungicide such as benomyl. Repot.
Wilted foliage, wet root ball, white roots	Sucking insects	Place the bonsai where the root ball drains well and stays warm from the sun. Start alternately misting the foliage with clear water one day and mild detergent the next. Remove any visible insects with tweezers.
Wilted foliage, wet root ball, brown leaf edges	Sun scald	Move bonsai into shade. Trim off dead parts of leaves and branches. Lightly fertilize and wait for new growth to appear.

Wilted foliage, wet root ball, discolored leaves, twig dieback	Blight	Trim away all dead and stressed areas. Treat with a systemic fungicide. Sterilize your tools. Plant bonsai in the ground away from other similar plants.
Twig dieback; other foliage is okay	Too cold last winter	Trim away damaged parts. Fertilize lightly and redesign bonsai to fill in bare areas with healthy growth.
Sudden color change on one branch	Virus	Trim away affected parts and sterilize your tools.
Yellow leaves, green veins	Chlorosis	Fertilize. Use plenty of water before and after. Reapply fertilizer in one week.
Yellow leaves and veins	Mineral deficiency	Apply a trace-mineral fertilizer that includes iron, sulfur, manganese, magnesium and zinc.
Tiny holes in leaves	Shot-hole fungus	Apply systemic fungicide.
Leaves chewed away	Insect damage	See the chapter on insects.
Top of tree is dying	Sunburn	Move bonsai to shade and mist foliage.
Bottom of tree is dying	Too much shade	Rotate your tree and prune away congested areas in the top. Fertilize lightly.
Pale color in conifer, dry root ball, tiny webs	Red spider mites	Apply miticide or ten applications of detergent solution at three-day intervals. Prune away heavy foliage. Place in warm, sunny location.
Holes in deadwood	Borers	Inject any insecticide into holes with a syringe.
Constant oozing of sap from wound	Borers	Clean off wound with turpentine. Inject insecticide into any visible wound holes. Apply systemic insecticide to entire tree.

Scum on trunk	Overwatering	Scrub off scum with toothbrush. Water roots only, not trunk.
Scum on deadwood	Rot	Apply full-strength lime sulfur with a small brush.
Scum on pot	Algae	Remove bonsai from pot. Soak pot in mild chlorine-bleach solution; drain and scrub. Apply a light mineral oil to pot, then repot.
White crust on pot	Mineral, salt deposit	Remove bonsai from pot. Soak pot in vinegar solution overnight. Scrub with brush and rinse well. Apply light coat of mineral oil to pot, then repot.
White crust on soil surface	Mineral, salt deposit	Soak bonsai pot and roots in shallow tray for one half hour, rinse well. Water more deeply in the future.
Green scum on soil surface	Overwatering	Check to see if roots are too crowded. In the future, water this bonsai only when surface is dry.
Liverwort in pot	Too much nitrogen	When applying fertilizer, wash off excess with final rinse. Don't apply slow-release granules to soil surface.
Insects in soil	Drain holes are no longer covered	Clean out empty pot and attach new soil screens with fresh copper staples. Sprinkle a few diazinon granules in bottom of pot, then repot.
Ants crawling over bonsai	Aphids	Treat foliage with detergent as you would for aphids. The ants indicate the presence of sucking insects.
Red leaves on green plant	Heat exhaustion	Move plant to a shadier location. Mist foliage; water well.
New buds fail to open	Phosphorus deficiency	Fertilize lightly with 0-10-10 and bonemeal.
Flowers fail to open	Potassium deficiency	Fertilize as above.

Flowers fail to produce	No pollination	It might have been too cold for the bees to do their work. If it's still not too late, irritate the remaining flowers with a small brush.
White powder on leaves	Mildew	Treat with systemic fungicide. Move bonsai to sunnier location. Water only in the morning. Trim away affected areas; sterilize tools.
Black spots on leaves	Fungus	Treat as above.
Rust-colored powder on leaves	Fungus	Treat as above. See the chapter on disease.
Sudden growth of large leaves	Excess nitrogen	Water your bonsai well to leach out excess fertilizer. Place bonsai in sunny location and trim off unsightly foliage.
Sudden foliage drop	Heat stroke	Move bonsai to shade, mist remaining foliage. Water well once, then water sparingly until recovery.
Leaves too small	Pot bound	Repot.
Leaves too small	Not pot bound; lack of nitrogen	Fertilize lightly.
White flecks on leaves	Scale	Touch fleck with a bit of mineral oil on a cotton applicator stick.
Flying dandruff	White fly	Apply insecticidal soap. See the chapter on insects.
New growth wilted	Winter damage	Check roots. If they look healthy, move bonsai into shade and water sparingly.
Last year's growth falling off	Too hot	Move bonsai to shadier location. Water well once, then sparingly until foliage stops dropping. Apply vitamin B-1 solution to root ball after one week.

One branch dies suddenly	Mechanical damage	Look for a break in the branch. Perhaps a falling object hit it or a cat jumped on it. Check also for wire damage. Trim off branch.
Large hole in soil	Squirrel or large bird	It may be necessary to wrap the bonsai with protective screen. Avoid feeding these animals with nuts and berries if possible. Sometimes a toy pinwheel will keep these animals at a distance.
Long, leggy growth	Not enough light	Move the tree to a sunnier location. Trim off unsightly growth. Pinch back new shoots often.
Blue conifer fading to green	Magnesium deficiency	Apply a pinch of Epsom salts to your liquid fertilizer. Blue color intensifies in sunny location. Make sure to give the plant enough light. Existing growth is difficult to change.
No flowers on tree	Incorrect pruning	If your tree is four years old or older, flowers will form each year. Heavy annual pruning will usually remove flower spurs. For best results, prune only after flowers fade.

Obviously I can't possibly anticipate every problem that might come along, but don't worry. There's a solution to every emergency situation. If you've gone through the preceding list, and you're still unsure of what might be causing the problem, or what the solution might be, here's what to do: Pull the bonsai out of its pot and place it on the bonsai shelf without its pot. With a moderate stream of clear water, rinse the foliage, branches, trunk and roots. While it is still dripping wet, place the root ball on the ground in your garden where you know the soil is free of pesticides. Don't dig a hole for the roots. Mound plenty of fresh compost over the root ball and water it thoroughly. Set a sprinkler nearby and, for the next three days, make sure the tree is watered well. After one week, apply a light application of systemic insecticide, together with a systemic fungicide. Some products combine them for you. Wait ten days and apply again. After two weeks, apply a low-percentage (3-5-5) liquid fertilizer. Grow this bonsai as a small shrub for as long as it takes to show healthy foliage and vigorous growth again; it might take one or two years. You can always repot it later. The important thing is that you've saved the tree. Keep your bonsai alive!

Chapter 11

SEASONAL CHECKLIST

Sometimes it's frustrating to read bonsai literature and come across an important point—a reminder to apply bonemeal in autumn, for example. Of course, you'll be reading the book in spring, so you try to remind yourself to store that advice until autumn. Most often, a bonsai doesn't die of one isolated neglected factor. A tree can be made stronger throughout the year with a regimen of timely watering, fertilizing and pruning. This same tree will withstand a greater range of hot and cold than would a similar plant that had suffered through yearlong neglect. You can point to the frost and blame it for the demise of your favorite bald cypress, but if you had known enough to withhold water from this delicate species in the autumn, you might have been able to make the bonsai more resistant to frost. Numerous examples could illustrate the intricate intertwin-

ing of the good general health of a plant and its resistance to insects, disease, and other natural calamities.

Remember that in the Southern Hemisphere the seasons are reversed. July in the United States should be converted to January in Australia. In addition, the strength of each season depends upon how far you live from the equator. Near the Arctic Circle, summer lasts only a few days. Conversely, winter is insignificant in tropical climates. I substitute seasonal designations for the names of the months in an attempt to make this chapter meaningful to all.

For most gardeners, the months of December, January, and February will translate to early winter, midwinter, and late winter. March, April and May will be called early, mid- and late spring. June, July and August are early, middle, and late summer. September,

October and November are early, middle, and late autumn.

If you live in a region near the 45th north (or south) parallel (as I do), these translations seem unnecessary. If you live farther north, as in Newfoundland, or farther south, as on the Baja Peninsula, I hope you'll appreciate this global approach to bonsai care. I offer the following "tags" to assist the reader in identifying the seasons with respect to their local environment.

Early spring	Cherry blossoms
Mid-spring	Maple leaves open
Late spring	Oak leaves open
Early summer	Pine forms secondary candles
Midsummer	Three-year-old conifer growth starts to drop
Late summer	Hottest days of the year
Early autumn	First color change in deciduous trees
Mid-autumn	First frost
Late autumn	Deciduous leaves all dropped
Early winter	Snow and persistent cold
Midwinter	Ice, long nights and short days
Late winter	Bulbs emerge from soil

These general descriptions will help you to understand and "calibrate" the following information. If the cherry blossoms in your area don't appear until April, no matter. Just follow the suggestions for early spring at that time. If you never get snow, just follow the suggestions for early winter, the month after all your deciduous tree leaves have dropped.

EARLY WINTER

✔ Prune autumn-blooming bonsai, for example, some magnolia, chrysanthemum, camellia or similar plants. New buds are formed in late spring, so severe pruning for shape must be done now in order to avoid "harvesting" next year's blossoms during spring pruning.

✔ Pay careful attention to watering. Always remember that one complete, useful watering consists of three consecutive waterings, even in winter. Light watering or incomplete watering only promotes mineral buildup in the container. If you water, then water thoroughly or not at all. Caution: The bonsai will form a natural canopy over the pot. Even in a downpour, the pot won't be watered sufficiently. Take advantage of this natural moisture and humidity. Water in anticipation of a great downpour and your bonsai will appreciate it.

✔ Clean pots of mineral residues. Pull the bonsai from the container and wrap the root ball in a saturated towel. Soak the empty pot in a shallow container of water and vinegar, then scrub the pot with a stiff brush. **Fig. 11-1.** Alternately soak and brush the pot until clean. Apply a light coat of mineral oil to the outside of the pot to restore the original patina, then repot. For severely calcified containers, it may be necessary to remove your tree into a temporary container. The calcified

Fig. 11-1

bonsai pot can then be planted deeply in the ground for a year. Soil bacteria and microorganisms will clean the pot thoroughly for you. Just remember where you buried it!

✔ Apply lime sulfur to deciduous trees. The simple application of a dormant spray is always underrated. Winter comes, the "bugs" aren't around anymore and the lax bonsai grower gets lulled into thinking that insect and disease problems have gone away. Winter is an ideal time for a preventive application of lime sulfur to your deciduous trees. Lime sulfur is a wonderful pesticide. It's made of lime and sulfur, not chlorinated hydrocarbons which pollute groundwater and are responsible for major problems up the food chain. Winter is your window of opportunity. Apply lime sulfur now and enjoy success next year. Ignore this chance and problems will come your way in spring. Follow the directions on the label. Don't allow the pesticide to drip into the bonsai container.

✔ No fertilizer. As in the previous month, no additional nutrition is needed for your plants. What nutrient the bonsai needs has already been stored in the plant tissues of the stems and roots. In addition, fertilizer delivered to the plant at this time would be wasted because of the low ambient temperature and the bonsai's lack of growth.

✔ Water early in the day. Overnight temperatures drop suddenly at dusk, creating a real problem both for bonsai and their pots. When water suddenly turns into ice crystals, a brief period of rapid expansion occurs. Water in a closed container, as in a cascade pot, expands quickly as the temperature decreases from 32°F (0°C) to 31°F (−1°C). This expansion is powerful enough to explode your bonsai pots. Similarly, excess water in your bonsai plant's vascular tissues at dusk can do irreparable harm to the natural veins that carry water and nutrition throughout the plant. Succulent white root tips are most susceptible to this exploding phenomenon during freezing. Early watering in the day provides the bonsai with the time necessary to rid itself of excess moisture before dusk. Early watering allows for tiny air spaces to be incorporated between soil particles. Minerals and starches have time to accumulate in the vascular tissues of the plant again, helping to protect the plant from freezing.

✔ Remove large clumps of moss. Excess moss in winter will harbor insects and disease. Excess moss will hold moisture content in the pot at a dangerously high level. Removing this excess vegetation will improve soil drainage, increase beneficial oxygen to the roots and warm the root ball by allowing the winter sun to contact the soil and container.

✔ Don't transplant trees. Repotting is always a traumatic event in the life of a plant. Broken root hairs won't have the ability to repair themselves because they aren't growing. The tree's natural immune system is down. Bacteria and fungus can successfully invade the plant. Root rot occurs as spring approaches. Better to let the bonsai rest without damage. Spring is just around the corner. Be patient.

✔ Collect rocks. **Fig. 11-2.** Rocks for rock plantings, landscapes, viewing stones and *saikei*. Look for the perfect rock to place under the exposed roots of a juniper or maple that you've been growing. Make plans for a root-over-

Fig. 11-2

rock planting, utilizing a young seedling you're developing.

✔ Disinfect your bonsai bench. Remove all trees from the bench and apply a solution of half water, half household bleach to the bench surfaces. A compressed-air sprayer will do a fine job. The strong bleach solution may spot your clothes and damage adjacent plants, so be careful during application. Scrub unusually slippery green or dark areas of the bench with a brush. Where water tends to stand, either tilt the bench or drill holes in it to improve drainage. After letting this water-bleach solution stand for one hour, spray it all clean with a good hard blast with fresh water from your garden hose. Wait one week before applying oil preservatives; the bleach will continue to work.

✔ Finish cleaning up fall debris. Pick up all leaves and needles from the bonsai soil surface. Pluck off any remaining leaves that continue to cling to their branches. Wipe off the bottoms of all your pots. Move your bonsai around on the bench to avoid discoloring one particular spot on the bench surface. Clean up your yard. Remove all debris that will decompose this winter. Falling twigs and branches from overhanging or adjacent trees harbor insects and disease that will attack your trees this coming spring. Thorough mulching is one solution; complete removal of these hosts is the other solution.

✔ Sketch your trees. **Fig. 11-3.** Bring your bonsai, one at a time, into your home. Put them on your best display stand and contemplate them for a while. I realize that most people aren't proficient pen-and-ink artists, but to deny that you have artistic skill means that you can't design bonsai. Make two drawings of each tree. The first drawing should be what you would like this bonsai to look like next winter.

Fig. 11-3

The next drawing should be what you would like the bonsai to look like in ten years. Save these drawings and look at them again next winter. Did you accomplish your goals? If you didn't, then do you know why? What are you going to do this year that you didn't do last year? Are you letting the tree design itself, or are *you* in control?

✔ Wire deciduous bonsai. After your maple or elm tree has been inside the house for a couple of days, it'll be dry and you'll need to take it back outside and water it well. Before you do, this is an opportune moment to wire and bend the branches. Wilted celery is flaccid and flexible; it can be easily bent without breaking. The branches of deciduous trees are similar. When fresh and loaded with nutrition and water, they're crisp and they'll break easily. After a few days in the house, the branches on a deciduous tree will be fairly supple and pliable, because they're partially wilted. This is an excellent opportunity to wind the branches with copper wire and bend them into the appropriate conformation without splitting or cracking them. The next day, the bonsai can be lightly watered to slowly return the branches to their normal turgor pressure. Don't water heavily immediately after wiring. Let the branches adjust slowly to their new positions.

✔ Read books, take notes, observe other bonsai and make plans for the future. Take advantage of the relatively slow time in your bonsai calendar to catch up on tasks that normally are placed on the "back burner." Use this quiet time to do the important developmental tasks that will propel you to the next higher level of success.

MIDWINTER

✔ Enjoy the indoor display of your bonsai. Nothing is quite as satisfying as a fine twiggy deciduous bonsai to greet you in the living room, or a shapely pine tree welcoming holiday guests as they arrive. Enjoy your trees as you share them with others.

✔ Bare-root broadleaf evergreens, if necessary. One of the disadvantages of growing camellias, rhododendrons, azaleas and similar plants as bonsai is that the broad evergreen leaf surfaces make them less dormant than other plants. The green leaves are present year-round and can capture the sun's rays at any time. As a group, they're highly successful plants. Just look around you in the winter and take note of the huge number of varieties and shapes. Some are trees, most are shrubs and hedges. A few ground covers even make good bonsai if trained up on a stake for a few years. Midwinter gives you a fine opportunity to drastically dig into the evergreens' root balls. Avoid cutting roots, if possible. For best results, alternate a strong water flow with combing action from a dull root rake or chopsticks. This drastic bare-rooting would be harmful at any other time of the year.

✔ Begin cold stratification of seeds. Most outdoor bonsai species require a period of moist cold before sowing. Place your seeds in a large kettle of warm water overnight. Crack open the shells of hard-coated seeds the next morning. Place the seeds in several moist handfuls of coarse sphagnum moss that's been lightly sprinkled with a fungicide. Place the moss and seeds together in a plastic bag and store them for the remainder of winter in the coldest part of your refrigerator. There's no need to freeze them. In early spring, wash and clean the seeds and sow in a coarse planting mix in a protected area, such as a windowsill or greenhouse. Transplant when the roots are 3″ (7.5 cm) long.

✔ Remove mistletoe. **Fig. 11-4.** While it may be unique and fascinating to have mistletoe on your oak tree, mistletoe is a parasite and it will weaken your bonsai. Removal is sometimes not

Fig. 11-4

enough the first time, but persistent removal will eliminate the problem. Please note that many high-altitude conifers collected from nature might also have this pest. Native materials should always be carefully checked over in their first few years in your garden. Avoid the spread of insects and disease. Even quarantine them if necessary.

✔ Don't fertilize this month. Check your soil carefully and examine its health. Watch for signs of alkali buildup, calcium residues, or salt. If you live in a place where the water is hard, add some soil sulfur to your bonsai soil every year at this time. If your water is soft, check for green slime, abundant moss growth and liverwort,

and for signs of acid soil or nitrogen buildup. Correct such soils with bonemeal, agricultural limestone or wood ash. The plant will perform noticeably better this coming year if you do.

✔ Water protected bonsai. Don't forget the plants that you've protected under your benches, or placed next to the house, or buried in a cold frame. It's easy to neglect them when they're out of sight. On warm, windy days, an extra dose of moisture will be appreciated. Avoid watering after noon.

✔ Check your stock of bonsai soil. Spring is coming soon. Next month bare-rooting season begins and the plants you'll bare-root will use up a lot of soil. Screen more soil if necessary. Don't run out of soil when your busiest transplanting season finally arrives.

✔ Prepare for a sudden cold snap. There's nothing as frustrating as sitting down to a warm evening meal inside your home only to hear the pop of an exploding cascade pot outside, or the beginnings of a hailstorm. Monitor the weather reports regularly and have backup systems for all your emergency equipment. Keep plenty of spare light bulbs, flashlight batteries, extension cords and plastic sheeting. You may have to suddenly move your plants indoors into your garage or utility room, so have the area clean and ready. Keep a few small folding tables or benches handy. In the event of a power outage, are your greenhouse plants safe or will you lose your whole crop? A portable generator or propane heater might be a good investment.

✔ First application of copper. Some growers prefer the use of lime sulfur as a dormant spray. Others prefer a copper-based liquid. I think both are equally effective. However, I've found that copper used throughout winter, beginning just after leaf drop in the fall, causes some trunk and branch discoloration, particularly in irregular or corky barks. In addition, the nice creamy white of zelkova, elm or birch can be darkened with repeated applications of copper. I find that if I restrict copper applications to mid- or late winter only, this darkening isn't noticeable.

✔ Plan for spring growth and make a list of the tasks ahead. Which trees must be bare-rooted? Which trees need transplanting? Which need to be transplanted from the ground into their first bonsai pot? Which trees will be grafted? Which will need drastic restyling? Prioritize your list.

✔ Sharpen your tools. Comparatively speaking, this season is the least busy, so this is an excellent chance to catch up on this often-neglected task. Charge into your spring projects with freshly sharpened tools. There will be no need to stop in the middle of a re-potting project to sharpen your root scythe or your concave cutters. Seek professional help if you feel uncomfortable sharpening tools yourself. Remember how happy you were when you made the first cut with your brand-new bonsai shears? Now you're willing to tolerate blisters on your hand and risk carpal-tunnel syndrome from using dull, rusty tools. Restore that "just new" feeling.

LATE WINTER

✔ Last application of dormant spray. Unseasonably warm days may cause quick swelling of tight buds on early-blooming deciduous trees and shrubs, such as quince. Don't risk damage to your beautiful flowers by applying dormant sprays too late. If winter bulbs are sprouting from the ground, stop any further dormant-spray applications. Ideally, you should have had time for four applications from last autumn until now.

✔ Gall aphid control. This month is the only time of the year when the gall aphid actively seeks a new home in your fir, pine, spruce or hemlock. If your tree has the characteristic signs of this pest, see **Fig. 7-11.** Several judicious applications of insecticidal soap will take care of this pest this month. If you miss this opportunity, you'll have to use a systemic insecticide, because the insect is well hidden and protected inside the tree for the rest of the year.

✔ Train conifers now. The sap in conifers, right now, is just starting to flow slowly. They haven't built up enough turgor pressure yet to expand their buds, however. This is an ideal time to bend, twist or shape large branches or trunks. Withhold water for several days, wrap the branch or trunk with raffia or floral tape for protection, then bend gradually with wire, clamps, or turnbuckles. You can accomplish astonishing results this month that would be impossible to obtain later in the year.

✔ Prune early-blooming deciduous trees. Soon their flowers will be opening up. When you prune now, not only can you prune for shape, but you can prune knowing where the flowers will be. There's already a difference in the size and shape between fruiting buds,

Fig. 11-5, and vegetative buds, Fig. 11-6, so you can determine how many flowers you'll allow to bloom. Too many blooms and the tree will suffer.

✔ First fertilizer of the year. Apply a light application of liquid 10-15-10 or similar fertilizer. Add a few drops of the liquid to a watering can full of

Fig. 11-5

Fig. 11-6

water that's been standing for a few hours. Apply this solution slowly to the moist bonsai root ball. Wait thirty minutes, then rinse your bonsai with fresh water.

✔ Bare-root conifers. This is an excellent time to transfer conifers from the ground into their first containers. Severe root pruning is acceptable now. Trim away a bit of foliage to compensate for the lack of roots.

✔ Beware of unusually warm weather. Check all your trees daily, especially after a bit of sunny or windy weather. Some pots will need moisture,

others won't. Don't water a moist bonsai.

Prepare beds for cuttings. As buds begin to swell, it will suddenly become perfect weather for taking cuttings. Prepare garden beds by mounding fresh soil into a raised row or between two large timbers. The increased drainage and air circulation will favor delicate new cuttings. If you prefer, use portable trays or boxes which can be moved about as the temperature fluctuates. I recommend this latter method if you have field mice, squirrels, or large aggressive birds around. A screen mesh of hardware cloth can be nailed to the top of your cutting box to discourage these pests.

✔ Graft this month. Sap is moving slightly, but so slowly that it won't interfere with the union of the scion to the stock plant. There are a number of ways to graft. Whichever method you choose, the cambium layers of both the scion and the host plant must precisely meet each other, and the cuts must be freshly made with an extremely sharp knife. Sealing the cut area will protect the graft until a callus forms and the wound can heal itself naturally.

EARLY SPRING

✔ Prune early-blooming deciduous azaleas and rhododendrons. The popular Exbury and Mollus azaleas will provide you with a spectacular show of flowers this month. Actually, there are quite a number of early-blooming shrubs that are good for bonsai, including forsythia, star magnolia, witch hazel, sasanqua camellia, quince, and wild cherry. As soon as the blooms

Fig. 11-7

fade, severe pruning back of the bonsai will restore its shape and still not harvest next year's blooms. **Fig. 11-7.** Pinch back new vegetative growth for two more months as it appears, then stop.

✔ Shape deciduous trees as they sprout. Once the basic tree outline is formed, maintain it by pinching back new growth regularly throughout the growing season. Next year, you'll be rewarded with a fine twiggy tree. Wire as necessary before new growth completely obscures your efforts.

✔ Check your wires from last year. If they won't accommodate this year's spring expansion, replace them now, while you can still see the branches. Test your wire clearance; you should be able to poke a wire between the branch and the training wire around it. If you can't, replace the wires now.

✔ Bare-root azaleas this month. Nursery azaleas that are potted for landscaping purposes are planted in a soil mix that's mostly peat moss. This mix is appropriate for landscaping use because the plant will be transplanted into the ground. For bonsai purposes, however, this soil is too short-lived. If you're developing a bonsai azalea in a bonsai pot, this is an excellent month to attempt to "comb out" as much of this peat as you can, without disturbing

the azalea's roots. You will, of course, tear some roots in the process. Don't tear too many at one time. You may have to finish the job next year. Try to incorporate as much coarse bonsai soil as you can between the roots. The pot will drain better and your azalea will develop roots that resemble those of a conifer rather than the typical spongy, amorphous roots that are found growing in peat.

✔ Plant root-over-rock projects. Comb out the roots of a three- to five-year-old plant and place them around a shapely, interesting rock. Lightly bind the roots to the rock, using floral tape or wide rubber bands. Plant the roots, rock and all, into the ground or into a large container. Grow for one more year, and then gradually start brushing away the soil from the top of the rock. You'll be well on your way to a stunning root-over-rock planting in just two years. Any other method is tedious and not as effective.

✔ Thread-graft this month; now is the best month. The terminal buds on conifers and deciduous trees are swelling and *committed* (meaning they'll sprout). Without damaging this bud, drill a hole completely through the trunk as small as you can. Secure the graft with a straight pin on the opposite side and wait. For pine, this graft will take two years. Maple will be ready by fall.

✔ Bring trees out of winter protection. Trees that have been stored in greenhouses will burn when exposed to the direct sun, so allow for a gradual transition. Deciduous trees that break their dormancy can be pruned back lightly and allowed to get used to the sunshine again. Don't prune off all spindly growth at one time. Eventually, however, it will all have to come off. Open the cold frame a little bit longer each day, especially in the morning, when the sun first starts to heat up the enclosed space. Transplant your ground-planted bonsai as soon as their buds start to show activity. Don't wait for new growth to appear; by then it will be too late.

✔ Adjust to unseasonably hot or cold weather. For hot weather, protect tender growth from sunburn. Water well but don't fertilize. For unusual cold snaps, move the plants back into the cold frame, garage, or unheated utility room. Withhold water and mound plenty of mulch over the soil. A bit of fertilizer added to the mulch will actually help heat up the root ball.

✔ Control growth by intentional wilting. As new growth emerges strong and upright, cut back on watering slightly until you see the first signs of wilting; then water sparingly. Repeat this process several times a week this month and your new growth will appear smaller, stronger and more compact. Unlimited water in the spring, by contrast, encourages large, long, upright and fragile growth that's best pruned away. Try intentional wilting whenever you can this month. Water carefully, or overwilting will cause damage.

✔ Set blossoms by hand if necessary. Sometimes, when it's warm, but a bit too rainy for the bees, pollination is spotty and fruit doesn't follow the flower. If these conditions are present when your fruiting bonsai comes into bloom, just lightly touch the inside of each flower with a small artist's brush. **Fig. 11-8.** This mechanical procedure

will allow pollination to happen without the bees, and your fruit will be set.

✔ Give a good dose of fertilizer at least twice this month. Water well, then apply diluted 5-10-10, or a similar

Fig. 11-8

formula. Wait thirty minutes and water well again.

✔ Trim off *water sprouts* as they appear. After severe pruning on a fruit tree, we're all familiar with the strong vertical shoots that appear later. These are sometimes called water sprouts because they appear after the spring rains begin. Actually, they're just strong new growth that's growing too fast to develop strength. They always appear after heavy pruning. The tree is attempting to quickly restore the balance between root growth and foliage growth. Remove buds immediately when they appear where they're not needed, as along the tops of branches. Thin out large clumps of buds that appear all around a pruning scar. Retain only one or two buds. As the new growth extends itself, prune it back to only one or two leaves. Prune so that you point the terminal leaf towards the direction in which you desire further growth.

✔ Transplant this month. I teach bonsai classes at a local community college. It's always difficult to get a full class this month. People usually don't want to think about gardening this early, yet this is the easiest and most practical time to do major potting, re-potting, styling, bending and pruning. My classes are always full one month later, when it's becoming inappropriate to do drastic work on plants. Try to get accustomed to working earlier in the year; your plants will appreciate it.

✔ Deciduous cuttings of stone fruits and flowering trees. Prepare cut-ting beds prior to taking cuttings. The secret to success is threefold. First, *tear* off cuttings rather than cutting them off with sharp scissors. This tearing helps to concentrate natural healing and growth hormones. Second, the ap-plication of rooting hormone and the movement of the cutting itself must happen in a matter of seconds, not minutes. For this reason, I find that a portable tray filled with sand or perlite brought right to the donor tree is use-ful. If you prefer growing your cuttings in the ground, either make the cutting bed right nearby, or bring the whole host tree over to the cutting bed and take your cuttings there. Third, the soil must be draining perfectly, so that you can lightly mist the fresh cuttings at will without danger of excess damp-ness.

✔ Evaluate each of your trees. About ten years ago, I had a most start-ling revelation. I was giving out good advice to students, but when I looked at my own trees, I was being soft and forgiving. I wasn't taking my own ad-vice! I was putting off projects for un-known reasons. We tend to accept ad-vice from others about our own trees, even when we know what we *should* be doing. Look at your trees this month with a cold, unforgiving eye. Some-times it helps to look at a photograph of your tree.

MID-SPRING

✔ Take cuttings of conifers. Place these cuttings into pure sand or perlite; soil won't drain well enough. In soil, your cuttings will rot before they root. I find that liquid rooting hormone works better than the powdered kind for conifers, and that a bit of DMSO (dimethyl sulphoxide) added to the hormone will drive it into the tough plant tissues a bit faster. Remember, with cuttings, speed is important. Cau-tion: Don't *ever* combine DMSO with a pesticide.

✔ Prune early-blooming bonsai. By now, your flowering cherry, apple, plum camellia, etc. have bloomed. **Fig. 11-9.** Trim back for general shape and thin out the branches before the veg-etative growth gets heavy. In areas where the sun won't penetrate, leaves will die.

✔ Twist off long pine candles. The presence of pine candles this early in-dicates strong hormonal growth. Re-move the strongest and longest candles this early to help redistribute growth

Fig. 11-9

throughout the plant. **Fig. 11-10.** Remember, growth hormones work in reverse. That is, the removal of strong growth means that you're removing a bud-inhibiting hormone (encouraging side shoots and small internodes). Remove the most powerful candles entirely. Don't make the mistake of retaining any part of the candle; growth will only be redirected to the remaining fragment.

✔ Begin pinching back new growth. A compact bud contains all the blueprints for a very long branch; make sure it doesn't extend to this length. During the growing season allow three leaves

Fig. 11-10

or three pairs of leaves to emerge from a developing bud, then pinch back to one leaf or one pair of leaves. With conifers, simply shape the new growth as it appears. Nip off the new growth while it's chartreuse and succulent. If you need to use a pruning tool, you've waited too long.

✔ Control slugs and snails. The wet spring weather will hatch thousands of new gastropods. Buy an inexpensive brand of beer and leave a few shallow containers of it lying around the growing area.

✔ Water rapidly growing bonsai only. The first sign of plant distress is that the root balls don't take up moisture in the spring. If you water randomly or universally over your collection, you won't notice your plant's distress call. Plants that remain wet in spring need to be treated with a fungicide and to be planted in the ground.

✔ Begin to rotate your plants. Turn them around on the bench. Let all sides enjoy the sunshine. The plants will develop in a more balanced and even fashion.

✔ Wire weak branches. If you're having trouble developing a lower branch, wire it up instead of down. Place this weak branch towards the sun to redistribute the balance of growth on your bonsai.

✔ Move your plants around to regulate growth. A maple that's producing leggy growth needs more sun, a sulking juniper needs more sun, a sunburned elm needs to be pruned back and placed in a shadier location. You can regulate water, growth and direction of development this month by moving your plants around, depending upon their individual needs. Allow plenty of space between bonsai. Due to lack of air circulation and sunlight, a crowded bench will be a diseased bench.

✔ Transplant pine, fir, hemlock and spruce. Don't bare-root, but transfer the root ball carefully from one container to another. Remove mud, silt, debris, and decaying organic matter. Rinse the root ball several times with a moderate stream of fresh water while the roots are out of the pot. Pine roots are well known for their close association with fungus called *mycorrhizae*. Always retain a bit of this whitish fungus and transplant some of it along with the roots. The relationship between fungus and roots is well documented in pine, but this same relationship occurs in other species, as well. I think we are just now beginning to understand and appreciate the importance of soil microorganisms. Try to retain a bit of soil mould when transplanting all trees; it seems to be beneficial.

✔ Watch for aphids. **Fig. 11-11.** New succulent growth this month will attract many kinds of sucking insects, including the ubiquitous aphids. Observe this new growth carefully and apply insecticidal soap immediately for quick and easy results. Once the aphid colony grows, removing it becomes far more difficult.

LATE SPRING

✔ Take cuttings of *kurume* and *satsuki* azaleas. If your cutting has a flower

Fig. 11-11

remnant on it or a lingering seed pod, pinch out such a remnant carefully. Always take more cuttings than you need, for they won't all sprout. You should get at least 60% of your cuttings to root successfully in one month's time. Transplant when the roots are at least 1½″ (4 cm) long; it should take about eight weeks for them to reach this length.

✔ Prune maples often. Wait until the third pair of leaves just starts to emerge from the new shoot, then prune back to only one pair. **Fig. 11-12.** To avoid scarring, remove unwanted new buds from the trunk as they become visible.

✔ Wilt conifers occasionally. New growth shouldn't always come out strong and full of moisture. Withhold water until the new shoots just start to droop, then mist the foliage. Water deeply the following morning. The process will strengthen the new growth, make it shorter, and decrease the size of the internodes.

✔ Check the drain holes in your pots. Pick up the pots and examine them carefully to see if the root mass is pulling the screens away from the drain holes, allowing insects easy access to the soil. A quick repotting may be necessary. Trim away excess rootage from the holes, since it will interfere with drainage. Look for signs of insects hiding under each pot. A light sprinkling of granular insecticide on the bench and under the pots will discourage crawling pests.

✔ Twist candles on pine. There are many ways to control the growth of pine. The most common method used is to twist off the majority of the longest candles and half of the medium-

Fig. 11-12

Fig. 11-13

sized candles, and leave the smallest ones alone. For a more complete description of this process, see *The Bonsai Workshop*, Sterling Publishing Co., Inc., 1994, pp. 107–111.

✔ Check wired branches. **Fig. 11-13.** Spring is almost over, but most wires should stay on for one more month. If the wires start to cut into the bark, they must be cut off. Don't twist off the wire; you risk severely tearing the bark.

✔ Repot late-blooming plants. Although they are few, there are bonsai that bloom in summer. This month is their springtime, so it's safe to transplant them now without damage.

✔ Tip cascading plants on their side. Many cascading plants, such as chrysanthemum, are hard to grow if you don't. Strong upward growth in a species usually means that lower branches tend to grow weak over time. This is a good month to invigorate

these lower branches by tilting the bonsai, so that the lowest branches are more upright and face the sun. I've even grown bonsai upside down!

✔ Prune according to visible vigor. Strong shoots must be pinched back hard and weak shoots should be rotated towards the sun and pruned back only lightly. Especially prune away unwanted growth that shades important branches.

✔ Watch for excess moisture during hot weather. This is the beginning of the mildew season. Fresh succulent, warm and wet growth is the first to get mildew. Water only in the mornings, especially if you know it'll be warm that day. Water all your bonsai well when it rains. Take advantage of the bit of natural moisture they receive and drench them thoroughly with additional water. Foliage tends to act like an umbrella over the pot. You think your plants are getting really wet, but they aren't. As a test, place a small can on the soil surface under the canopy of a bonsai. Compare moisture in this can with a similar can out in the open. You'll be surprised at the difference between the two cans when you compare the water levels in both.

✔ Start training tender new growth immediately. If you wait until midsummer to train new maple branches, you'll find that they're brittle and they'll break off easily. If you wait until next year to train them, you'll get a rather weeping appearance near the trunk. You'll no longer be able to get that nice precise downward angle found on old bonsai specimens. Carefully loop a wire around the new growth this month and gently tease the young branch down into place by fastening the other end of the wire to the pot, a root or even to the bench itself. This type of wiring is the gentlest method I know. If you tie down a branch to the bench, don't forget that it's tied there when you rotate your tree!

EARLY SUMMER

✔ First opportunity to treat *jin*, *shari* and *saba-miki*. **Fig. 11-14.** This month, the average temperature will rise enough so that the lime sulfur will be able to soak into the driftwood areas on your bonsai. In cooler weather, the lime sulfur concentrate tends just to coat these surfaces, and the end result looks more like white paint than sun-bleached driftwood-grey. Pour a small quantity of the undiluted concentrate into a small glass container. Dip a small artist's brush in the liquid and carefully paint all dead areas on your tree. After forty-eight hours, the dead wood will be silvery grey and well preserved for another season. Apply additional coats as needed. Refer to **Figs. 8-2, 8-3, 8-4.**

✔ Select second-growth candles on your pine. **Fig. 11-15.** By now, your earlier pinching and twisting of the first candles has forced some new growth to begin. Rub out unwanted buds as soon

Fig. 11-14

as you can, without damaging adjacent desirable growth. Use tweezers if necessary, because fingers can be somewhat large and clumsy in cramped situations.

✔ Pinch back growth on high-altitude conifers. For a few years just after collection, these trees will break their buds at nearly the same time that they would have in the wild. These later-

Fig. 11-15

growing conifers will gradually adjust to lower elevations. For the first few years, however, give them extra time to extend their new growth. Don't pinch them back in spring, but wait until early summer.

✔ Leaf-trim deciduous trees. The first time I saw someone do this to a maple, I was skeptical, but it really works! Just make sure you're doing it for the right reasons; the tree should be healthy, bonsai styling should be

90% or more complete, the leaves must be on a young, vigorously growing tree, and the leaves must seem to appear to be too large. If any of these conditions are absent, standard pruning is best. Remember to use a very sharp scissors and cut halfway between each leaf bud and its branch attachment. The remaining leaf stem should be allowed to fall off by itself. Carefully monitor water uptake for the first few weeks after defoliation. The tree can't use water as rapidly without its leaves. This isn't a good time to rot its roots. In a few weeks, you'll get tiny, perfectly shaped leaves that will give you a spectacular autumn display.

✔ Prune rhododendrons and azaleas. Any spring-blooming bonsai can be pruned back safely this month. There are still enough long days left in the year so the plant can reset new flower buds for next spring.

✔ Pinch back oak. **Fig. 11-16.** The first strong shoots of oak should be appearing now. To avoid excess elongation and large leaf size, pinch back these strong shoots to only one leaf. The secondary shoots will appear smaller, and two of their leaves may be kept. Judge the severity of pruning necessary by observing leaf size. Retain small leaves. Heavily trim shoots that

Fig. 11-16

produce large leaves.

✔ Thread-graft this month, just as you would in spring. Pull off all the foliage that's in the way, even on conifers. Save an intact terminal bud and push the branch through the hole and secure it as you would in spring. New growth will arrive quickly.

✔ Avoid watering at midday. This is the beginning of summer, when the combination of moisture and heat can cause sun scald and mildew. Water early in the day. If an additional watering is needed, wait until after 4:00 P.M., but not as late as dusk. On a really dry day, water everything, whether it needs it or not. Broadcast a large, fine stream of water over the foliage, branches, bench, pots, under the benches and nearby structures as well. The additional humidity and coolness will linger longer around your half-baked plants. Don't do this every day.

✔ Watch for borers, thrips and mites. The warm weather will bring out all kinds of insects. Check all your trees as you water each day. Don't let a week go by with these insects on the loose, for they multiply quickly.

✔ Transplant trees only on rainy days. If emergency repotting must be done, wait for an unusually cool or overcast day. If such a day doesn't come, transplant indoors and leave the plant inside until an overcast day comes before moving it out. Protect recent plantings by putting them under the full shade of a tree.

✔ Remember to train by intentional wilting. This process was described last month.

✔ Air-layer trees this month. Cut a wide swath that completely circles the trunk. Make your cut deep, beyond the cambium layer. Wrap the bare area with premoistened sphagnum moss and then wrap the same area with clear plastic, then black plastic. With this method, you can open the black plastic and check for white roots showing against the clear plastic.

✔ Select fruit for display. **Fig. 11-17.** By now the blossoms on your fruiting bonsai are all faded away, and the fruit is starting to expand as it grows its seeds and protective pulp and skin. There's no point to keeping one hundred tiny kumquats on your citrus tree; it will only endanger the health of the bonsai. Prune away unneeded fruit. A good bonsai display will have only fifteen fruits on a 20″ (8 cm) tree. Remove excess fruit now, so that the tree will be stronger.

Fig. 11-17

MIDSUMMER

✔ Remove large amounts of copper wire. Copper wire conducts heat extremely well. Unfortunately, this property turns copper wire into a liability in the hottest summer months. To the detriment of the bonsai branches, the sun's heat is passed along these coils of wire encircling them. Aluminum also makes good bonsai wire. If you have a tree that's been trained heavily with wire, I suggest removing most of the wire during the summer. Moving the tree to the shade will stop the excess heat, but will elongate the new growth of the tree. Better to remove the wire.

✔ Treat *jin, shari* and *saba miki* this month with lime sulfur. The heat will help the chemical penetrate the deadwood.

✔ Remove third-year growth from conifers. At this time of the year, needles that are three years old will naturally start turning yellow and they'll begin to fall off. If you rip these needles away, you'll be stimulating the formation of new buds for next year. Conifer buds form where sunlight touches the branches, particularly where injury has occurred. By tearing off old needles now, you can help stimulate a tremendous crop of new buds for next fall.

✔ Remember to rotate your trees. Your trees will perform considerably better if you rotate them on a regular basis.

✔ Watch for signs of heat stress. Excess heat can cause burned leaf margins, unusually small new leaves, wilt, and scorched leaf surfaces. Keep a careful eye out for these signs. If a tree has been holding out well without damage, reward it with a few days' vacation in the shade.

✔ Fertilize this month with fish emulsion. The trace minerals in this organic slurry will benefit heat-stressed plants. Apply the emulsion with plenty of water before and after each application. Fertilize only on cloudy, overcast days.

✔ Last month to defoliate. If you trim off deciduous leaves completely any later, you might not have enough warm days left in the year to replace them with new growth. In warmer climates such risk is not as great.

✔ Prune flowering and fruiting trees with respect for next year's bloom. Learn how to identify the different growth characteristics between flowering and vegetative growth. Each species is slightly different. Judicious pruning at this time will keep you from limiting your blossoms next spring. In general, prune for compact growth and close internodes. The outside shape of the bonsai must be maintained. Limit the inside growth to enable strong branches to receive sunlight. Any other pruning or thinning may remove next year's fruit and flowers.

LATE SUMMER

✔ Control secondary growth of maples. **Fig. 11-18.** Most deciduous trees will experience a short summer dormancy period during which new growth

Fig. 11-18

is temporarily arrested. On unseasonably cool summer days, or during rainy weather, these trees will react as if spring has arrived again. Trim the new shoots just as you would in spring.

✔ Water often and water deeply. Use a sprinkler, if necessary, to broadcast a lot of moisture around your bonsai. As always, avoid midday moisture.

✔ Apply 5-10-10 fertilizer, trace elements and Epsom salts. Autumn is coming and these nutrients must be in the soil in advance, allowing the tree to store valuable minerals and carbohydrates for the colder season. Three small applications of any and all of these substances this month are much better than one large dose.

✔ To prevent and remove algae from bonsai that are getting lots of water, such as elm, birch and zelkova, scrub the trunks clean with a toothbrush dipped in a dilute solution of lime sulfur. **Fig. 11-19.**

✔ Protect trees from afternoon sun. When the temperature is hot, give your

Fig. 11-19

trees some shade from 1:00 to 4:00 in the afternoon. Monitor local weather reports for unusually hot days. If you go on vacation, make sure your neighbor or alternate caretaker is aware of this potential problem.

✔ Let your bonsai enjoy the remainder of the summer. Give them plenty of water and rest from constant sun. Fertilize sparingly, trim only when necessary, rotate often, wire with caution and remove yellowing needles and leaves as they appear. Repot only in cases of extreme emergency.

✔ Prune to avoid dieback. Pretend your eyes are the sun and look over your trees from top to bottom. Rotate the trees on a turntable. If you can't penetrate large clumps of growth with your vision, these areas must be trimmed back, because shaded parts of the plant will weaken and die. One overactive branch can kill the branch below it and start a chain reaction in which the tree designs itself, instead of you designing the tree.

✔ Cut pine needles in half to promote secondary budding. In young, vigorous trees and in long-needled pine species, shorten the pine needles by cutting them in half. This cutting process is temporary (the needles will fall off, anyway), and only for long-needled pines or for rapidly growing pines in training. Bunch up the pine needles over next year's bud and trim straight across all needles, avoiding the buds underneath. New buds will be stimulated because of the increased amount of sunlight that touches the branch. Brown needle tips, after pruning in this manner, can be minimized by lightly misting the foliage regularly over the next few days.

EARLY AUTUMN

✔ Plant root-over-rock bonsai, rock plantings and *saikei*. **Fig. 11-20.** Autumn is a time of limited foliage growth and the beginning of a prolonged period of root growth. Take advantage of this season to create complex plantings that would be difficult to achieve in spring, when stored root energy is ready

Fig. 11-20

to be expressed as foliage growth. When creating rock plantings, the primary goal is to establish the root mass; this is the appropriate month for this.

✔ The last application of fertilizer that contains nitrogen. With all nutrients, try to anticipate growth. You won't anticipate significant growth next month; therefore, don't apply nitrogen after this month. You can, however, anticipate the continued formation of next year's buds and autumn root growth, so the best fertilizer is a 3-10-5, or something similar.

✔ For better autumn color, restrict water on deciduous trees. Once the leaves on a maple or elm turn color, they're essentially dormant; they've shut down. Sugars and minerals take over the job of maintaining these deciduous trees. Autumn color in Vermont is spectacular partly because of the lack of heavy rain during this month. In Oregon, where I live, I can reproduce these colors by restricting water on my deciduous bonsai. The autumn color in Oregon is limited to just a few days because autumn rains turn everything to brown, but my bonsai retain their brilliant color longer, due to the intentional limitation of water.

✔ Water selectively. Like spring, autumn produces conditions which favor some plants but not others. Actively growing conifers use moisture at a rate much greater than deciduous trees do that are just going into dormancy. Water these two types of bonsai differently. Don't overwater or underwater.

✔ Transplant deciduous trees. One distinct advantage of autumn color is that it indicates when it's safe to repot. If the tree shows any color at all, it's safe to transplant it. Take advantage of this opportunity to repot; it won't happen again until early spring.

✔ Excellent time to collect trees from the wild. The color change in maples indicates a good time to collect deciduous trees, and conifers, as well. Plan a nice autumn excursion into the countryside. You'll enjoy beautiful autumn color, ideal mild temperatures, and the knowledge that these trees that you dig will survive the ordeal!

✔ This month marks the season when outdoor temperatures closely resemble indoor temperatures, an excellent time to bring these trees indoors. Before you do, prune away leggy growth and with the sharp blast of the hose nozzle, remove dust. Prune away yellowed leaves and dead twigs. Make sure the tree is insect-free before including it with your other healthy indoor bonsai.

✔ Prepare winter storage. It may seem too early to perform these tasks, but I've found it far more pleasant to build cold frames this month than wait for the weather to turn frosty. Plan ahead to make these tasks easier. Remove thermometers, extension cords and plastic sheeting from storage. Take an inventory of what you'll need.

✔ Watch for autumn pests. Each year, I seem to get an extraordinary invasion of blue jays, crows, opossums, and squirrels during this month. Take steps to control these animals. They're preparing for winter just as you are. To prevent the damage that these animals can do in a relatively short period of time, be vigilant.

✔ Slugs and snails increase their presence as autumn rains arrive. Just as in spring, place a few shallow containers of beer in strategic locations around the yard.

MID-AUTUMN

✔ Prune autumn-blooming bonsai. Many rhododendrons, azaleas, chrysanthemums, and other plants are just now losing their blooms. As the flowers wilt, the plant will adjust its energy into setting seed. If these seed casings aren't removed now, this energy will be misdirected. Harvest some seed now, if you wish, but the focus of energy should be redirected towards winter survival and next spring's growth.

✔ Plant bonsai seeds outside. For gardens that experience winter snow, planting maple, pine, juniper and hemlock seed couldn't be better than now. The autumn rains will soak the seed coat. Winter frosts will crack the hard protective casings, and warm spring rain will germinate the seed. If you have natural pests, you may want to sow this seed in a protective box, instead of directly in the ground.

✔ Apply bonemeal; the trace minerals in it are varied and complex. It will benefit the roots of the plant as well as the future blossoms. Gently scrape the bonsai soil surface and water in about one handful of bonemeal for each 30″ (12 cm) plant.

✔ Begin autumn cleanup. Pick up fallen leaves as soon as you can. Remove these to a mulch pile or haul them away. Move the bonsai around on the benches to prevent algae from forming under the pots. A final spray of fungicide will protect the autumn leaves of citrus and stone-fruit trees.

✔ Water only as needed. The bonsai that are still growing will show dryness. Ignore the others. Don't water everything just because it's convenient.

✔ Protect all tropicals. By now, all semi-indoor bonsai should be in their winter quarters indoors. An overnight frost could damage them severely.

✔ Transplant and root-prune pre-bonsai growing in the ground. Go through your collection of bonsai that are in the ground and examine their roots. Prune away heavy, long roots and maintain short, compact, white root hairs. Loosen the ground all around the planting area. Remove weeds, moss and small stones. Replant the potential bonsai a bit higher than it was before. Mound soil generously around the trimmed root ball and water well.

✔ Check branch wires again. At this time of the year, there's another surge in branch diameter. The plant is storing sugars and starches for the winter; its reserve energy causes its tissues to swell quickly. This may be the best time to rewire bonsai, because you can take this swelling into consideration and allow for the future expansion of spring growth.

✔ Fertilize with 0-10-10. Autumn color will improve, root development will be enhanced, and spring buds will be more numerous.

LATE AUTUMN

✔ First application of lime sulfur. As the leaves on the deciduous bonsai fall, clean up the debris immediately. Maintain the ultimate in cleanliness around your benches. Water only when necessary and use forceful jets of water to clean off foliage and residues under the pots. Pick off the last half-dozen lingering leaves on your maples and apply the first dose of lime sulfur as soon as you can. Don't allow the spray to drip into the pots; it's toxic.

✔ Take photographs and make drawings of your trees. This will be the first opportunity to compare them with previous records from last year. Are your deciduous trees getting thicker trunks? Are they getting the beautiful twigginess so important to the illusion of age?

✔ Make preparations for alternate storage of bonsai. Your cold frames should be ready. Your benches should be prepared for you to place bonsai under them in the event of frost. Your seedling and cutting beds are protected. Your sensitive species should all be inside the house. What if there were a hailstorm tonight? Have you made contingency plans for your valuable trees?

✔ No wiring, no fertilizing, no transplanting, no collecting, no pruning. This just about sums up late fall. Divert your attention to the things that you can control. Your pine will appreciate unseasonal sun. Group together those trees that require similar winter care. Construct new benches for next year. Build outdoor stands for better display. Read a new bonsai book.

Cryptocarya	B	J	R	U	Y
Cryptomeria	D	H	R	U	Y
Cuphea	A	K	P	U	Z
Cupressocyparis	D	H	R	U	Y
Cupressus	D	H	R	U	Y
Currant	C	J	R	S	Y
Cycas	C	M	R	U	Y
Cytisus	B	K	P,Q	U	Y,Z
Daphne	B	K	R	S,T,U	Y
Echeveria	E	O	R	–	Z
Elaeagnus	C	K	R	S,U	Y
Equisetum	A	O	R	–	Y
Erica	B	K	R	–	Y
Eugenia	B	K	P,Q	S	Z
Euonymus	B	K	R	S	Y
Eurya	A	K	P	S	Z
Fagus	B	K	R	S,T,U	Y
Ficus	B	N	Q	U	Y,Z
Forsythia	B	L	R	S	Y
Fraxinus	C	M	R	S,T,U	Y
Fuchsia	B	K	Q	S	Y
Gardenia	B	J	Q	S,U	Y
Ginkgo	C	K	R	–	Y
Guaiacum	A	K	P,Q	S,U,V	Y,Z
Gymnocladus	B	M	R	S	Y
Hedera	B	K	R	S	Y
Hibiscus	A	K	P,Q	S	Y,Z
Ilex	C	K	R	S,U	Y
Ixora	A	K	P,Q	S	Y,Z
Juniperus	E	H	R	U	X
Kalmia	A	K	R	S,U	Y
Laburnum	B	M	R	S,T,U	Y
Lagerstroemia	C	K	R	S	Y
Larix	D	I	R	U,V	Y
Laurus	B	K	R	S,U,V	Y
Lavandula	B	J	R	–	Y
Leptospermum	B	K	R	S,U	Y
Leucothoe	A	K	R	S	Y
Ligustrum	B	K	R	S,U	Y
Liquidambar	C	K	R	S,T,U	Y
Lithocarpus	B	K	R	S,U	Y
Luma	C	J	R	U	Y
Macadamia	A	K	Q	U	Y,Z
Magnolia	B	K	R	S,U	Y
Malus	C	L	R	S,T,U,V	Y
Melia	C	J	R	U	Y
Metasequoia	A	I	R	U	Y

Morus	B	K	R	U	Y
Myrica	B	K	R	S	Y
Myrsine	B	K	R	S,U	Y
Myrtus	C	K	R	S	Y
Nandina	A	O	R	—	Y
Nicodemia	B	K	P	U	Y,Z
Nothofagus	B	K	R	—	Y
Nyssa	B	K	R	S	Y
Olea	C	K	R	S	Y
Osmanthus	A	J	R	S,U	Y
Oxydendrum	A	J	R	S,U	Y
Parrotia	C	K	R	S	Y
Pelargonium	A	K	P,Q	S	Y,Z
Photinia	B	M	R	S	Y
Phylica	A	K	P	S	Z
Physocarpus	B	K	R	—	Y
Picea	D,E	G	R	U	X
Pieris	A	K	R	S,U	Y
Pinus	D,E	F	R	U	X
Pistachia	B	M	R	S,U	Y
Pittosporum	B	M	R	S,U	Y
Platanus	B	K	R	S,T,U,V	Y
Platycladus	D	H	R	S,U	Y
Plum	C	L	R	S,T,U,V	Y
Podocarpus	C	M	Q,R	S,U	Y,Z
Polyscias	A	J	P	S	Z
Populus	B	K	R	S,T,U,V	Y
Portulacaria	E	N	Q,R	—	Y,Z
Potentilla	B	K	R	S	Y
Prosopis	D	K	R	U	Y
Prune	C	L	R	S,U	Y
Prunus	C	L	R	S,U	Y
Pseudolarix	D	I	R	—	Y
Pseudotsuga	D	G	R	U,V	X
Psidium	A	K	P,Q	S,U	Y,Z
Pumica	C	J	Q,R	S,U	Y
Pyracantha	C	L	R	S,T,U,V	Y
Pyrus	C	L	R	S,T,U,V	Y
Quercus	E	K	R	U	Y
Raphiolepsis	A	K	P,Q	S,U	Y,Z
Rhamnus	C	J	R	S,U	Y
Rhododendron	A	L	R	S,U	Y
Ribes	B	K	R	S	Y
Rosa	C	L	R	S,T,U,V	Y
Rosmarinus	B	K	Q,R	—	Y,Z
Salix	B	K	R	S,T,U,V,W	Y
Salvia	B	K	R	—	Y

Sambulus	B	K	R	S	Y
Schefflera	A	M,N	P,Q	S,U	Y,Z
Schinus	C	M	R	U	Y
Sciadopitys	A	F	Q,R	S,U	Y
Sequoia	A	I	R	S,U	Y
Serissa	B	K	P,Q	U	Y,Z
Sophora	B	K	P,Q	U	Y,Z
Sorbus	C	M	R	U	Y
Syrax	B	K	R	S,U	Y
Syringa	A	K	R	S	Y
Syzygium	C	K	R	S	Y
Tamarix	B	M	R	S,U	Y
Taxodium	A	M	Q,R	S	Y
Taxus	C	G	R	U	Y
Thuja	D	H	R	S,U	Y
Tilia	B	K	R	S,U	Y
Trachelospermum	A	K	P	S	Y,Z
Tsuga	D	G	R	U,V	X
Ulmus	B	K	R	S,T,U,V	Y
Vaccinium	A	K	R	S,U	Y
Viburnum	B	K	R	U	Y
Weigela	B	J	R	S	Y
Wisteria	B	L,M	Q,R	U	Y
Wrightia	A	K	P,Q	S,V	Y,Z
Zelkova	B	K	R	S,T,U	Y
Ziziphus	C	K	R	S,T,U	Y

A Soil Type This soil type is ideal for those small trees and shrubs which grow under the canopy of larger trees. The taller trees shed their leaves and needles each year, forming a rich blanket of compost on the forest floor. This relatively thin layer of humus supports a large variety of deciduous and evergreen shrubs and small trees. The roots of these plants tend to be shallow, finely textured and rather spongy in appearance.

The largest part of the soil should be made up of aged woody products, such as bark, sawdust, hardwood chips, leaf mould, and the like. Add about 20% soil vermiculite, mica, cat litter or other inorganic soil amendment to provide some mineral source and to increase sustained friability of the mix. Transplant or repot these species often, because the high-organic soil content decomposes rapidly.

B Soil Type This soil is made for common deciduous trees; they're similar in their needs and habitat, and they're found at most altitudes wherever moisture is available on a predictable basis. They're quite seasonal and, therefore, thrive in moderate to cold climates. Their roots stretch out considerably in their quest for both moisture and nutrients. Transplanting is required after just two years.

Mix this soil with about 60–70%

coarse peat, bark, rotted hardwood chips or aged sawdust, all carefully screened to remove smaller particles. Add to this a healthy dose of mineral supplement: coarse sand, decomposed rock, mica, perlite, vermiculite, hard clay or pumice. The tree's roots will encircle the inside of the pot quickly, so check the pot's drain holes frequently.

C Soil Type This soil type is reserved for the tough fruiting and flowering trees that grow in nature in miserable soil. These trees aren't pampered, as delicate as their blooms are. We find them growing in spartan conditions in the wild: along rock ledges, in high plains country, and as impenetrable thickets. They're loved for their blossoms and their fruit, but they shouldn't be pampered.

Their soil mix should be well screened. For maximum drainage, use only the coarsest materials. A good balanced blend of organic and inorganic sources is best. Coarse peat should be used sparingly in favor of wood chips and bark that won't decompose as rapidly. Similarly, leaf mould, in about a year, will make the soil too heavy. Mix in a generous amount, up to 60%, of coarse mason's sand, cat litter, decomposed granite, pumice, lava cinders, or vermiculite. The roots of these trees don't care to be disturbed, so make your soil coarse enough not to have to transplant for three years after repotting. An annual application of bonemeal is imperative.

D Soil Type This soil type suits most conifers, including deciduous conifers found in nature at higher elevations. Hardy evergreen shrubs that line gorges, beaches, and windy cliffs also like this mix. These trees are sun-tolerant plants that thrive in wind, rain, snow, and mild drought. They're found at all elevations, from sea level to 4000 ft. (1020 m).

These plants grow primarily in rock that has decomposed over time. Between 60 and 70% of their soil should contain sand, perlite, vermiculite, mica, pumice, volcanic ash, lava cinders or crushed rock. These plants need a small portion of their soil made up of organic debris, however. Add some leaf mould, rotten needles, old sawdust or a combination of bark and manure, but add them sparingly and mix them well into the soil. The roots of these plants tolerate a bit of surface exposure and will form nice character if allowed to grow bark. Transplant these trees every four years.

E Soil Type This soil is best for high-altitude desert plants, such as cactus, succulents and drought-tolerant species. These plants are nature's wonders. We see them struggling against all adversity on mountains, cliffs, and arid stretches. They survive because of their ability to shut down during hard times. When moisture is present and conditions are favorable, they have the ability to quickly break dormancy and take advantage of the opportunity to grow.

The bulk of this soil mix is decomposed rock of some kind. Try to collect this rock when you visit the desert or mountains. It may be pumice, sandstone flakes, mica, vermiculite, coarse sand, lava cinders or volcanic debris. Add only enough needles, leaves or mulch to make the soil complete. This soil type only needs about 10–20% of these organic components.

F Pruning Technique The pine family grows by sending out annual new growth called a "candle." **Fig. 12-1.** Without damaging adjacent candles, remove dominant candles in their entirety as soon as possible in early spring. The remaining candles are allowed to lengthen until the individual needles just start to separate from each other. If it's large, most of this candle should be gently twisted off. If the candle is medium-size, pinch off only half. If the candle's small, allow it to grow.

Fig. 12-1

G Pruning Technique In this family of plants that includes spruce, fir and hemlock, **Fig. 12-2,** new early-spring growth is protected by a sheath. When this thin covering falls off naturally, you'll see an oblong-shaped concentration of bright green, new needles trying to unfold. Remove all these buds in their entirety; they're young and tender. Grasp them between thumb and forefinger and gently pull forward without much force and they'll separate. This early-spring pinching will start a series of efforts by the tree to grow. New growth will appear everywhere. Pick and choose the buds that you desire and rub out the buds that you don't want.

Fig. 12-2

H Pruning Technique This technique is appropriate for most of the needle junipers, cypress, cedar and arborvitae. **Fig. 12-3.** New growth appears in mid-spring and it is characterized by the gradual appearance of a light-chartreuse–colored growth on the outer extensions of the branches or apex. To stimulate lots of new buds within the branch, allow this growth to continue until it is about 1″ (2.5 cm) long, then completely remove it. This pruning technique requires you to prune constantly during the growing season, even up to early autumn.

I Pruning Technique Prune these deciduous conifers only after the branch has grown about 2″ (5 cm) in length. **Fig. 12-4.** Early-spring growth is too succulent to shape or wire. Rub out unwanted buds as soon as they appear. Allow branch growth to extend

Fig. 12-3

Fig. 12-5

Fig. 12-4

several inches (cms) before pinching back the tip; the branch will then divide. Secondary growth should be allowed to extend for 2" (5 cm) before pruning again; then this branch will divide once again. Give these plants as much sun as they can stand without burning them. Bright sunlight will help compact new growth.

J Pruning Technique This pruning is appropriate for any deciduous tree that grows leaves opposite one another along the branch. **Fig. 12-5.** The new growth in spring will produce a regular, predictable pattern of leaves. Two leaves will first appear as a curled-up clump of foliage, which will then open up. The next two leaves will appear shortly after, but rotated 90° along the branch (with respect to the first two leaves). Select the pair of leaves which are growing horizontal to each other instead of vertical to each other. Prune just in front of them when the branch

extends itself further. Before cutting, make sure that new growth has extended itself at least two pairs of leaves beyond where you want to cut, enhancing *back-budding* (the ability of a tree to expand advantageous buds). If you prune after only one pair of leaves has emerged beyond the pruning site, new growth will only occur at the branch tip. If you wait until the third or fourth pair of leaves appears, the internodes will be too long.

K Pruning Technique These deciduous trees have alternate leaves along the branch. **Fig. 12-6.** The leaf direction indicates the future direction of the new bud. If you don't want growth upward, for example, don't prune just beyond an upward-facing leaf stem. If you desire growth to extend towards the right, prune just beyond a leaf that faces in that direction. You'll find that leaves will sprout in a very regular fashion: up, down, right, left, up, down, right, left. There will be plenty of opportunities to sculpt your tree properly.

L Pruning Technique This very specialized pruning technique is appropriate to any of the rose family (including the blackberry, wild rose, cotoneaster, pyracantha, apple and dogwood, among others). **Fig. 12-7.**

Fig. 12-6

Fig. 12-7

Nothing will happen. You must wait until this tree produces another series of "leaves" beyond the first series before you have two real leaves. Then prune off one of these to get the branch to divide.

Fig. 12-8

Fig. 12-9

The pruning of this group requires that you study the differences between vegetative and fruiting growth. Fruiting growth, unfortunately, always appears on aging vegetative growth. You must maintain some select vegetative growth, or no fruit will appear. I recommend heavily pruning half the branches on the tree each year. The following year, prune back the other half. You can tell by the shape of the new growth which branches were pruned last year, allowing you to avoid pruning away blooms and blooms in progress.

M Pruning Technique These trees produce what looks like a number of leaves on a branch, but they actually produce only *one* leaf! **Fig. 12-8.** Their "leaves" are really a cluster of what look like individual leaves, but they're not. Don't make the mistake of thinking you can control growth by pinching or pruning between these "leaves":

N Pruning Technique This method is used on tropical trees having milky latex sap. **Fig. 12-9.** Growth is constant, since these trees are typically grown in rather sheltered locations such as greenhouses or atriums. Don't use a sharp pruning tool; you'll make the plant "bleed" excessively. Use a dull knife, poultry scissors or a wire cutter. On large specimens, I prefer to prune with needlenosed pliers because the pruning injury is great, therefore creating a massive load of traumatic acid in the plant. Healing is stimulated by the trauma and the sap loss stops. An extremely sharp knife will cause a maple to produce gallons of sugary sap, but the blow from a dull ax will readily heal over. The same principle can be applied to these tropicals. Did you ever notice how long it takes to heal a cut from a razor blade?

O Pruning Technique These bonsai are members of the grass, lily or tuber family. **Fig. 12-10.** They're propagated by division. To improve style, pruning consists of removing distracting growth. When old growth becomes yellow and unproductive, use root trimmers to remove it below ground level.

Fig. 12-11

Fig. 12-10

P Indoors or Outdoors These plants grow near the equator. **Fig. 12-11.** They don't desire to feel seasonal change. They want a constant source of bright indirect light and a modest fluctuation in temperature, from 80°F (27°C) during the day to 50°F (10°C) at night. They grow constantly and must be pruned constantly. Their leaves require copious quantities of water, nutrients and oxygen. They abhor movement, and putting them in a new location will send them into temporary shock. Don't touch them, because the skin on your hands has oils that will damage the leaves.

Q Indoors or Outdoors These plants, from near the equator, feel the

Fig. 12-12

seasons, but they won't tolerate frost. **Fig. 12-12.** In colder climates, these plants can become temporary house guests during winter. Strong sunlight through a window is tolerated because they've spent the summer outdoors. In late spring, move them outdoors again, trim off the gangly growth that occurred during their indoor stay, and gradually acclimate them to the sun again.

R Indoors or Outdoors These plants are native to colder climates. **Fig. 12-13.** They constitute, by far, the largest group of bonsai, perhaps around 90%. This group includes most conifers and all deciduous trees. Because they're in containers, protect them from extreme heat and extreme cold.

Fig. 12-13

S Common Pests These plants are highly susceptible to aphids, whitefly, thrips, mites, mealybugs, and other soft-bodied insects. The plants' succulent new growth is easy prey for these insects, which are looking for a source of sweet sap. **Fig. 12-14.**

Fig. 12-14

T Common Pests These are water-loving deciduous trees. Beginning in late spring and extending to midsummer, caterpillars are always a threat.

U Common Pests These plants are prone to attack by a group of insects known by their protective coatings or armor, including spittle bugs, scale insects and woolly aphids, among others.

V Common Pests These plants will likely experience an attack of boring insects. This group of insects includes the tiny pests that burrow into deadwood. Insects that hide at night inside the tree are also included in this category, since the treatment is the same. **Fig. 12-15.** See chapter 7.

Fig. 12-15

W Common Pests Protect these plants from slugs and snails. Their foliage is very tasty to these creatures; measures must be taken to prevent extensive damage to the plants.

X Sunlight Tolerance This group of plants will enjoy sun all day long.

Unusual circumstances may require shade, for example during your vacation, or in unusually hot weather. For the most part, however, let them bask in the sun's rays year-round. Rotate the plants to even out the strength of new growth. Avoid watering the foliage, except for an occasional cleansing blast from the garden hose. **Fig. 12-16.**

Fig. 12-17

Fig. 12-18

Fig. 12-16

Y Sunlight Tolerance This group of plants doesn't like the full heat of the summer sun after 1:00 P.M. The leaves will curl, turn brittle and scald if exposed to such strong light. Once the thermometer rises above 85°F (30°C) these plants prefer the mottled sun/shade found under the spreading canopy of a large shade tree. Give these plants plenty of water in the hottest months. Rinse off the foliage weekly. **Fig. 12-17.**

Z Sunlight Tolerance This group of plants would prefer never getting the

sun's direct rays. These plants, in nature, grow deep in the forest with plenty of moisture and humidity. Bright, indirect light from the sun is ideal. Temperatures between 65°F and 80°F (18°C–27°C) are preferred. Sometimes the addition of artificial grow lights is necessary for success. Don't place these plants out in the sun for any reason, not even for a few minutes; they'll burn quickly. **Fig. 12-18.**

Index

Care
  Autumn 81–83
  Spring 70–77
  Summer 20–26
  Winter 27–30
Care, Summer 20–26, 77–81
  Container Size 20
  Day, Length 24
  Humidity 21–22
  Location 22
  Plant Health 22–23
  Planting, Type 24–25
  Pot-Bound 23
  Seasons, World 22
  Shade 20
  Species Vigor 23–24
  Styling Considerations 25–26
  Temperature 21
  Tree Age 23
  Watering Frequency 20–21
  Wind, Prevailing 24
Care, Winter 27–30, 64–69
  Burying 27–28
  Location, Yard 27
  Mulching 29
  Sheltering 29–30
Common Names 6
Compact Moss 19

Diseases 47–51
  Algae 49
  Bench Cleaning 48–49
  Compost Process 47
  Herbicides 18–19
  Lichens 51
  Moisture, Excess 47
  Mottled Leaf 51
  Mould, Mildew 49
  Root Rot 50
  Shot Hole 40–50
  Sunburn 51
  Trunk, Cleaning 47–48
  Trunk, Keeping Dry 49
  Watering Times 49

Emergency Treatment 57–62
  Causes, Possible 58–62
  Checklist 58–62
  Inspection 57–58
  Observation 58–62
  Treatment 58–62
  Unpotting 62

Fertilizers 53–56
  Applying 55–56
  Ingredients 53–54
  Liquid, Solid 54
  Nitrogen 54
  Phosphorus 55
  Potassium 55
  Siphon 55

Hemispheric Seasons
  Chart 63–64
Herbicides 18–19

Indoor Bonsai 5, 8–9
Insects 39–46
  Boring 42
  Caterpillars 40–41
  Control 46
  Gall Aphids 43–44
  Self-Protected Pests 41–42
  Slugs, Snails 42–43
  Soft-Bodied, Sucking 39–40
  Spiders 41
  Weevils 43

Latin Names 6, 84–88

Outdoor Bonsai 5, 6–8
Outdoors or Indoors 5–10

Partially Outdoor Bonsai 8
Pests 96–97
Plant Identity 5–6
Preserved Plant 5
Problems, Nonproblems 44–46
  Altitude Change 45–46
  Color Change 44
  Lichens 51
  Moth 44
  Mottled Leaf 51
  Needle Droppage 44
  New Growth Coloration 46
  Resin Flecks 44
  Wind Damage 45
Pruning 37, 92–95

Repotting 31–38
  Aesthetic Purposes 35–38
  Algae 33, 34
  Hosing Roots 33
  How to 33–34
  Pot Size 33, 37

Root Congestion 33
  Tests 31–32
  Tools 31, 37

Seasonal Checklist 63–83
  Early Autumn 81–82
  Early Spring 70–73
  Early Summer 77–79
  Early Winter 64–67
  Hemispheric Seasons 63–64
  Late Autumn 83
  Late Spring 75–77
  Late Summer 80–81
  Late Winter 69
  Mid-Autumn 82–83
  Mid-Spring 73–75
  Midsummer 79–80
  Midwinter 67–69
Soils 52–53
  Ingredients 53
  Making 52–53
  Screens 52–53
  Types 90–92
Species Checklist 84–95
  Indoors/Outdoors 93–94
  Pests 94
  Pruning Technique 90–93
  Soil Types 90–92
  Sunlight Tolerance 94–95

Watering 11–16
  Devices 15–16
  How to 11–16, 49–50
  Frequency 20–21
  Importance 11
  Quality 15
Weeding 17–19
Weeds, Varieties 17–19